SO WHAT ELSE IS NEW?

SO WHAT

ELSE IS NEW?

by Hy Gardner

Illustrated by Sheila Greenwald

Prentice-Hall, Inc.
Englewood Cliffs, N. J.

To My Wife,
MARILYN,
who has done some
pretty peculiar things
herself—including marrying me.

Preface

I WAS PERCHED, rather comfortably, I thought, on Mike Wallace's television hot seat. This is reputed to be a piece of modern furniture that has burned more people in public than the electric chair has singed sinners in private.

Then Mike turned on the juice.

"Why! why!" my prosecuting attorney friend said shrilly, pointing his tongue at me, "did you, in your column of October 29, 1958, as a respected and highly quoted syndicated columnist, dare to palm off such ridiculously trite items as: 'The bellboys at the Diplomat Hotel in Hollywood, Florida, refuse to wear striped pants. . . . A boy born during a cocktail party on the third floor of the Stork Club eleven years ago still gets a case of champagne every birthday from Sherman Billingsley. . . . There are 19 restaurants in Manhattan named the Original Joe's—yet the founder of the Original Joe's was named Sam!' "

"Why! Hy, Why!" Mr. D.A. demanded, "with all the

weighty matters going on in the world, did you print such weightless material?"

"Mike, my dear boy," I said affably, seeking a reprieve from my executioner, "you pulled an ancient trick from out of your sleeve. You quoted out of context. You went people-trapping. You left out the title of the column from which you extracted excerpts. If you look at the original column of October 29, 1958, you will note that it refers to the contents as 'small talk,' in small, not even capital, letters. This format provides a change of pace patter, a release from the usual-unusual gossip, anecdotes, news tips, opinions, and inter-views we've been logging for the past 25 years. Why didn't you pick on our interview with Dr. Schweitzer? Or Maria Callas? Or President Syngman Rhee of Korea? Or a few of our news beats?"

Mr. Wallace, probably the best broken-field runner in the tevee game of tackling interviewees, abruptly switched to another question. But his query stuck in my mind.

The very premise of a celebrity column is people. Because people are interested in people—famous people for fame's sake, unknowns for the news they make. People do funny things, say amusing things under unamusing stress, get into untenable situations and sometimes act hilariously trying to extricate themselves. The strange behaviour makes filler fod-der for the greatest newspapers and wire services. It makes plain people celebrities for one or two editions, before they take cover under the blessed blanket of oblivion.

I thought to myself, munching on a hot dog between Mike's studio and the Trib office around the corner, that, for as long as people instinctively laugh when someone slips and falls or gets caught in a goofy situation, they'll like to hear about strange and unexpected doings, even though the doings have nothing whatever to do with balancing the budget or building world peace. By the time I reached the office, I had the notion tucked away in my mental tickler file.

Since I'm not especially ticklish, that probably would have been the end of the trail if I hadn't gotten a telephone call to meet some of the Prentice-Hall boys for a drink. They, it turns out, had the same idea in mind. They thought I ought to compile my favorite wacky-weird items into a book.

Sooooo, what else is new is this book.

It was written strictly to provide you with some chuckles, some conversation pieces, a few hours of light reading, and an opportunity to meet a horde of fascinating people, most of whom I'll guarantee you'll never meet or hear about again. The only thing weighty about this book is its bulk. I think it weighs around 14 ounces.

HY GARDNER
New York City

[EDITOR's NOTE: the exact weight of this book, as certified by Schultz's Meat Market, is 15 ounces, 3 grams, without thumb.]

Contents

CONTENTS

Introduction,
by Ed Sullivan

For the past quarter of a century, Hy Gardner has been an urbane resident of Broadway. Soft-voiced and with a ready smile, he just doesn't square with TV and movie caricatures of hard-boiled newspapermen, but this gracious veteran is a top-flight reporter, of the old school. He's always reminded me, in manner, of Jim Kilgallen, Dorothy's pop, who is equally gracious but equally singleminded when he gets his teeth into a story.

So What Else Is New?, his series of amusing illustrations that newspaper truth is forever stranger than fiction, is Gardner at his whimsical best. Hy has collected, in these pages, wry and amusing stories that newspapermen at city desks all over the country have used as one-column boxes or amusing fillers in daily papers, as a contrast to the ponderous international stories of friction.

I think that his selection of these stories is the best index to Hy Gardner's own jovial sense of humor. Of the hundreds of stories he has chosen, each fits neatly and amusingly into the categories of marriage, TV, police, traffic, lawbreakers, etcetera. Actually, he's been doing this sort of thing for years, from the days he was writing for *Parade* and the *Brooklyn Eagle,* and he is an expert at it, as you will discover to your own enjoyment.

His expertness is the result of Hy's continuous deep and friendly interest in people, all sorts of people. He knows all of the top names of our country and yet he never has been betrayed into the attitude of a "name-dropper." He just likes people.

And I'm glad that over the years, he's continued to like me and has permitted me to pen this foreword. Let's now open his book and enjoy ourselves.

SO WHAT ELSE IS NEW?

1

Wheeeee – the People!

In scanning the thousands of items that make the news, an odd-story collector quickly comes to one conclusion: people themselves are the most endlessly fascinating subject in the world. No mere novelist could invent the kind of situations that ordinary people constantly get themselves into—and out of. And certainly no professional gag-writer could come up, day after day, with the lines that spring spontaneously to the lips of harassed humanity.

The humor in these situations, of course, is often unconscious, and isn't necessarily very funny to the one involved. There was, for instance, the plight of the small boy in a crowded elevator in a Montreal department store. As the elevator rose, a woman suddenly screamed blue murder. "What happened?" the operator asked, bringing the car to a stop. A rather tall woman, red-faced and upset, massaged her rear-end but didn't say anything. It remained for a small-ish boy, standing directly behind her, to explain the shriek. "I did it," he said. "She pushed it in my face, so I bit it."

1

The remark broke up the other people in the elevator, but the diminutive culprit continued to stare defiance. I've always felt that that small boy was an eloquent symbol of all the people who have had to fight their way through life.

Another conclusion also forces itself on the odd-item collector: there are only so many basic jokes or situations. The only elements that make a joke or an incident appear fresh is a different name and a switch on one of the original patterns.

Of all these basic categories the one that, strangely enough, seems to breed the most humorous oddities is the Law. And that holds true from the local level all the way up to the F.B.I. In fact, one of my favorite items is the result of some sleight-of-hand thinking by these national cops. I heard it from J. Edgar Hoover, the Chief himself. It concerns the time the notorious Roger Touey gang broke out of Joliet prison in Illinois, during World War II.

The prison officials appealed to the F.B.I. to help in the search for the mobsters, but since it was a state, and not a federal matter, there was no way in which the G-men could legally participate. Finally, a Hoover aide came up with the loophole. The F.B.I. issued warrants for the arrest of all the escapees on the charge of changing their address without first notifying their draft boards.

In the same category, but all the way at the other extreme, was the excuse offered by the inebriated gent who was picked up by a Dayton, Ohio, squad car for wandering about the streets all night. "If I had any good explanation," he told the desk sergeant sadly, "I'd have gone straight home to my wife."

Later on in the book you'll find a chapter devoted to the wackiness of law and litigation, but I'd like to give you one more example that has always brought a smile to my face for some reason that deponent knoweth not.

Back in the days when Senator Estes Kefauver put his name in contention for the presidency through the televised Kefauver Committee hearings, he became the subject of many editorials, even in prison newspapers (yes, they have them). One such publication offered unarguable advice on the subject of prison reform. "Kefauver's on the beam all right," it said. "How can we ever expect to see any prison reforms until society begins to send a better class of citizen to jail?"

The subject of sex, of course, offers a large amount of the ridiculous to salt the daily round of living. The trouble with sex, though is that you're never sure if what you hear is true. Or, if it is true, is it true in just the way you hear it? There was no question, however, about the truthfulness of one clever item I saw recently—it was written down.

Bennett Cerf reported that a Kinsey-ish type of questionnaire was forwarded to Harvard grads in preparation for a twenty-fifth reunion. One alumnus refused absolutely to fill in the form. "In my opinion," he wrote in the margin, "sex is a subject to be discussed with women, not with an International Business Machine."

As an example of the kind of sex story that constantly reaches my ear, giving me a kick, but leaving a nagging doubt as to its veracity, I cite the following:

A maid in a wealthy home, an unmarried girl of 19, tearfully told her mistress that she was pregnant. Anxious to keep the girl and to help her through her distress, the

couple agreed to adopt the illegitimate infant. Next year, same situation, same solution. A couple of years later, ditto. Finally the maid quit. "I'm sorry," she explained, "but I can't work in a home where there are so many children."

Anyway, whether it's true or not, that's a pretty good sample of the kind of upside-down, double-take stuff that the nation's newspapers hungrily seek out to lighten their front pages. This kind of story never reaches the headlines, of course; it twinkles at you from the bottom of the page. But it tells, for me anyway, a hilarious story of the unpredictable side of human nature, and shows how crazy life can be for us ordinary guys.

Take the subject of *excuses*. All of us, whether we know it or not, are forever offering excuses for something we did, or failed to do. We're convinced, naturally, that our reasons are always good and sufficient to account for whatever it was that needed excusing.

It's not until we run up against an item like the following that we might possibly pause to consider our own conduct. A young Virginia lifeguard got into trouble not so long ago when his wife drowned in the bathtub. He explained that he was watching TV at the time, and said, "I guess I wasn't paying much attention to her. It was my day off."

See what I mean? People just automatically seem to reach for an excuse. Whether it's a carry-back to childhood insecurity or whatnot, I don't know, but even the wildest excuses seem to manage a tinge of *possibility*. There was a hill-billy down in Gadsden, Ala., who was hauled into court for failing to send his five children to school. "These kids like to use chawin' t'bacca and the teacher jest won't put spittoons in the classroom," he told the judge earnestly.

Not all of the items in this book were picked up from newspapers. Quite a few of them came to me from people who are just as intrigued as I am with the wacky behavior and roman candle activity of commoners. One such, I remember well, came to me from New Orleans' popular Abe Shushan. Abe reported seeing a sign in a ladies' shoe store that panicked passersby. It read: "French heels . . . Ideal for Street Walking."

Since, in my business, a lot of stuff like this comes my way, and some of it, at least, should be preserved for posterity, I have sprinkled it here and there throughout the ensuing chapters.

As I said above somewhere, after 20 years or so of bumping up against the weird behavior of ordinary people, it becomes

5

clear that there are less than a couple of dozen different basic situations or categories. Accordingly, I have organized the ingredients for this book into 17 chapters, chopping the meat to make it all palatable and enjoyable. But, so you'll get some idea of the kind of meatball mélange that's waiting for you, here are some random oddities that I have plucked as personal plums.

❖　❖　❖

Comedian Henny Youngman picked this up while working in a New Hope, Pa., nightclub. He didn't specify what small town newspaper was involved, but after the obituary editor died his son took over and signed the listing "Son Of Obituary Editor."

❖　❖　❖

Back in the days when I conducted "Hy Gardner's Newsreel" for *Parade,* Arthur "Red" Motley's fabulous Sunday newspaper supplement, I did an entire roundup of causes for divorce. Here are some of the oddest: Every once in a while when she was irritated she'd wait until he fell asleep, spread blonde hairs on his jacket, then wake him up and accuse him of cheating. Whenever he wanted to go out with the boys, he'd fake a telegram from her mother, reading, "Come immediately, am dying." To keep her spouse from going out, another woman hid her husband's false teeth. Still another witch tried to prevent her hubby from bowling with the boys by stuffing the holes of his bowling ball with cold cream. Then there's the woman who had a genuine gripe. Her husband kept filling her perfume atomizers with gin.

The divorce court in Cincinnati, Ohio, was the scene for a

rather unusual case. The wife of one young husband complained he constantly humiliated her. Whenever he invited out-of-town friends for dinner he dressed and addressed her as "the maid" so she could accept tips which he would wrest away from her after the company left.

❖ ❖ ❖

On the other hand, this one amused even the bored clerk in a Los Angeles courtroom. When a local woman discovered that her marriage wasn't legal, instead of trying to legalize it she filed suit against her "husband," demanding he pay her $24,000 plus interest for eight years work as housekeeper, secretary, nurse, cook, and concubine.

❖ ❖ ❖

A Detroit hackie, arrested after a crash when an inspection revealed a machine gun in his trunk, said he always took the weapon to work because he didn't want his kids to play with it in the back yard.

7

❖   ❖   ❖

Another inside story of convicts (incidentally, I musn't use that word too much; convicts prefer to be called prisoners) cropped up in South Walpole, Mass. Here the editor of the jail's weekly newspaper did an editorial suggesting that the boys keep smiling. "Do that," he wrote, "and all the guards will wonder what you've been up to."

❖   ❖   ❖

This incident also had a certain amount of inventiveness to it. A New York gambling ring was smashed when its rolling bookie room was arrested for speeding. The "room" turned out to be a used ambulance still bearing the identification signs of the hospital from which it was purchased. The driver wore a white jacket—with complexion to match!

❖   ❖   ❖

Here's one that came out of the recent political switchover in Cuba. A uniform maker who specializes in designing such attire for Latin American countries, approached Fidel Castro shortly after the revolution and showed him some new designs he had prepared for Cuban army, police, and government officials. When he got to one particularly flashy uniform, Castro blinked. It had yellow trousers with a blue stripe, a red jacket with gold epaulets, red shoes, and a yellow hat. "What is this for, señor?" he asked, "the Palace Guard?" "No, no," the tailor rejoined, with a slightly offended tone, "it's for your Secret Service men."
Olé!

❖   ❖   ❖

If I *had* to pick a favorite from the thousands of items I've seen in the past few years, I think it would be this one:

The story bears an Associated Press dateline from Boyne City, Mich., and I'll reprint it verbatim. "A 165-pound St. Bernard dog was revived with a slug of brandy after a search party from Boyne Mountain Ski Club found him lost in a snowstorm."

❖   ❖   ❖

So, there you are. And I now invite you to reel through the following hectic chronicle of humanity in its oddest and most outrageous moments.

2

Excuses, Excuses, Excuses!

WHETHER it's ingratitude, greed, laziness, or just a plain hankerin' to stretch the truth till it snaps right back in the fabricator's snout, there's no doubt about the truth of that durable proverb, "One excuse is as good as another."

Most people can produce plausible reasons for anything from passing a stop light to why their hands happened to be in a cash register in a darkened store at 12 midnight. It's a universal trait to look for excuses that will put our actions in a more acceptable light, and though we may be only kidding ourselves, there always seems to be a grain of *possibility* in even the wackiest excuses people think up.

The wife of one of the country's top golf pros probably comes closest to saying just what we mean. Her husband was frequently accused of telling white lies about his golf disasters. "He isn't a liar," she explained, "he just exaggerates awful big."

Maybe so; at any rate, he isn't the only one. Let's take a

look at some of the "awful big exaggerations" palmed off by people-on-the-spot.

❖   ❖   ❖

In Miami, tellers were concerned over a shortage of a pack of twenty $50 bills. They counted and recounted all night long to find the missing $1,000. When the bank opened in the morning a vice-president's new secretary, a pretty but rather dumb blonde, strolled in and asked why everyone was wearing such a long face. When the reason was explained to her, she smiled, opened her purse and gave the missing sheaf of bills to her boss. "I'm sorry if I caused such a fuss," she said, "but I just took these home to show mother the kind of work I was doing!"

❖   ❖   ❖

The editor of an Idaho weekly newspaper increased the dimensions of his tabloid sized page to a standard eight column size. An editorial explained the change was made to accommodate subscribers who only bought the paper because it gave them something to wrap around their whiskey bottles.

❖   ❖   ❖

There are hundreds of ridiculous excuses given by prisoners thwarted in attempts to escape jail, but the fellow who told this one deserves honorary membership in the National Liars Club. The attempted jailbreak occurred in a Hartford pen. Denying that he had any such silly idea in mind, convict Charles Blover seriously told authorities that the reason he had tied all those bedsheets together was because he was learning how to braid hair.

❖　❖　❖

In Rochester, N.Y., a taxpayer who failed to attach a withholding statement to his income tax return told a Revenue agent, "My 9-month-old son ate my W-2 form."

❖　❖　❖

In Memphis, Tenn., a girl who filled out her own form more satisfactorily than her tax form got into a hassle with the Revenue boys. Under the category "Property Improvements" she listed $500 spent with Slenderella to lose 20 pounds.

❖　❖　❖

Quite the reverse, a gal in Oakland, Calif., stuck a .38 in a bus driver's ribs and demanded that he drive without stopping to her place of business. "I was told," she told police, "that if I was late again I'd get fired."

❖　❖　❖

And in Detroit, a Lothario who was getting married for the fourth time without bothering to get a divorce from either his first, second, or third spouse, indignantly gave the court what he considered a valid excuse. Claiming it wasn't necessary to get a divorce, he showed the judge his latest marriage license, then pointed to a line in small print that read "This license void after two years." (Actually, the phrase quoted was intended to restrict the execution of the license to the period specified.)

❖　❖　❖

And a grim resident of North Plainfield, New Jersey, told doctors that the reason he shot himself in the stomach was to take his mind off a toothache.

❖　❖　❖

In Berkeley, Calif., a resident was called to explain his failure to pay a traffic fine. "I intended to," he said, hurt at the thought that he was a scofflaw, "but I gave the cash to my wife to use as a down payment for a divorce."

❖　❖　❖

In the Bay Ridge section of Brooklyn, a young man was arrested for drawing mustaches on all the faces of all the girls on all the subway posters. "Something inside made me do it," he told the judge. "You see, your honor, I'm a barber out of work."

❖　❖　❖

And an Appleton, Wis., dairyman, arrested for watering down the milk, said the milk was warm and he just spilled a couple of quarts of ice water into it to cool it.

❖　❖　❖

Of like mentality was the San Francisco man who, on a bet, bought fire insurance on a case of fine Havana cigars, smoked them, then, demanded the company return the cost of the burned property. They acceded, but had him arrested on charges of arson.

❖ ❖ ❖

A house-to-house vacuum cleaner salesman in Providence, R.I., accused of making improper advances to a housewife, tried to demonstrate to the court that it was an integral part of his sales technique. He got 10 days' time in which to change his technique.

❖ ❖ ❖

In Madison, Wis., police arrested a 76-year-old woman and her 82-year-old male companion on a charge of being drunk and boisterous. "We're sorry," the two of them apologized, "but we were on our first date and got all excited."

❖ ❖ ❖

Brought before the Alpena, Mich., court, a man accused of burning his house down denied it vehemently. To prove his innocence of that devilish deed he explained he was in Detroit the day in question, stealing a car.

❖   ❖   ❖

On the subject of car-stealing, a lawyer in Tel Aviv, defending a client who stole an automobile, told the court that that was impossible because Israel is too small a country for a vehicle to be stolen permanently. The court agreed and re-arrested the man on a charge of using a car without the owner's permission.

❖   ❖   ❖

Have you ever been bothered by telephone pests? Well, in Norfolk, Va., a pest was picked up for just taking numbers at random and picking up conversations with strangers. He admitted his guilt, saying: "My psychiatrist told me to meet new people."

❖   ❖   ❖

A Seattle teenager set a barn on fire to see if his girl friend and boy friend were two-timing him. "I was too bashful to knock," he explained, "and anyway I figured the fire would smoke them out."

❖   ❖   ❖

At the Marshall Field store in Chicago a male shoplifter was caught with six bras and five pairs of flimsy panties stuffed inside his windbreaker. "I intended to buy them for my girl," he told detectives, "but I get embarrassed when I ask salesgirls for this sort of feminine stuff."

❖   ❖   ❖

Apprehended on a charge of selling three cans of lager to a 10-year-old girl, a Madison, Wis., saloon-keeper said: "I thought she was 12."

16

❖　❖　❖

And in Milan, Tenn., state troopers picked up a drunken driver who told them that although his breath smelled like he was inebriated, he was perfectly sober—he just took a little brandy to deaden a toothache. Would have gotten away with it, too, excepting he smiled when he thanked the cops and they noticed he was completely toothless.

❖　❖　❖

Another drunk was picked up in Jacksonville, Fla., charged with stealing a cab. When asked if he had anything to say before being jugged he told the judge: "I sure have. I didn't steal the cab. I merely accepted their offer on tevee. Their slogan is 'When you drink too much take one of our cabs.'"

❖　❖　❖

A pink T-bird, speeding at 90 m.p.h. and turning corners on two wheels (even wilder than the usual Los Angeles-driven car) was finally slowed down by a motorcycle cop. A pretty young thing smiled and said: "I hope you're not mad with me officer, dear, I know I was naughty—but I just washed my car and had to go fast to dry it!"

❖　❖　❖

A Cincinnati tire robber was asked how come he was riding around on three stolen whitewall tires. "That's a logical question," he admitted, "and I have a logical answer. I found one tire, and needed three others to match it."

17

❖ ❖ ❖

Even more logical than this explanation was that given by a car thief in Fort Worth. He said he saw the car in front of a cemetery and assumed the owner was dead.

❖ ❖ ❖

If you're the type who always thinks of a witty retort after it's too late to make it, you'll admire the Montreal motorist who got a ticket in the midst of an election campaign. When charged with failing to signal that he was about to make a left turn, he told the traffic cop, "I was afraid that if I put my hand out of the window some candidate would shake it."

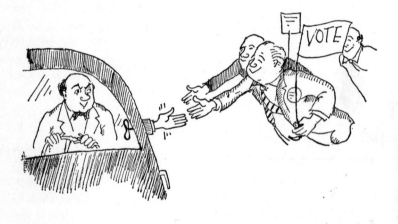

❖ ❖ ❖

Some stories, palmed off as being factual, stretch the imagination beyond the point of belief. Yet, when you're a collector of stories reflecting the unbelievable behavior of people, you wouldn't doubt the veracity of *any* story. This

18

is especially true if the yarn is spun by a professional story teller who repeats it so often he actually is ready to swear it's the truth, the whole truth, and nothing but the truth. Take this incident, for instance, and if you take it you take it right out of our column, just as two other columnists have already done.

It's all supposed to have started in front of the Waldorf. A mink-befurred, lorgnette-dangling dowager, with trunks stacked up like planes over Idlewild, was helped into a cab while a second cab took care of her excess. Her excess luggage that is. "Mrs. Whittlestick," the uniformed doorman said, "wishes to be driven to Pier 86, she's sailing on the S.S. United States." The hackie nodded, dropped the flag and took off.

In no longer than it takes to read a union contract, the cab arrived at the pier and the passenger spoke up. "If you're single and want to double your income, I'd like to offer you a proposition to see the world through your own windshield. How would you like to drive me around Europe, all expenses paid?"

The hackie's mouth opened, but no words came out. Finally, he nodded. In a few minutes arrangements were made to have the cab hoisted into the hold of the ship, where it remained till the ship berthed in Le Havre. From there they drove to Paris, then Nice, then Monte Carlo, then back to Le Havre for the channel crossing to England, then to Rome, Berlin, and through the Scandinavian countries. Like the cab's two occupants, the meter never stopped running.

Eventually the party retraced its tire treads, the United States docked again at the point of origin, Pier 86, the cab was hoisted out of the hold and plunked on terra firma. "Well, my good man," the fatigued dowager sighed, paying the $12,457 clicked on the clock, "we're on native soil

3

Ain't That the Limit?

IT TAKES all kinds of people to make a world, and, in the business of filling a yawning column of white space day after day you constantly run into the oddballs. Fortunately you meet most of the screwballs through the mails. They drop in daily for a three, four, or seven cent visit—by postcard, first class, and air mail.

Sometimes, if they really have something weighty they wish to get off their chests, and are allergic to various antihistamines, the squares take to sending telegrams or even making long distance telephone calls—prepaid. We seldom pay any attention to such messages. Any nut can cloak his identity or disguise his voice over a 'phone. You get so you can almost smell a crank call, letter, or wire.

My secretary is instructed to tell such callers, "Would you mind saying what's on your mind in writing?"

Invariably the callers aren't writers. They may be lonesome Georges or Janes who enjoy the vicarious thrill of scolding or correcting a columnist, and never consider the suggestion that they write a rebuff.

Those who do write generally are angry at something we reported or quoted, blaming us for making the news rather than recording it. They want to Be Shown. Which reminds us of the time Jayne Mansfield toured the state of Missouri to plug a movie, and then sent us a wire saying she finally found out why they call it the "Show Me" state—that she counted no less than 24 nudist colonies within its borders.

❖   ❖   ❖

Here are some examples of "Show Me" questions aimed in our direction:

"If, as you say, gambling is honest in Nevada, why does anybody lose?"

"Is there any truth to the rumor that when Sammy Davis, Jr., retires from show business he'll become a rabbi?"

"When Jack Paar has Elsa Maxwell on his show is it true that his cameramen are instructed to use wide-angle lenses?"

"Is Dody Goodman really a socialite who just went into television on a dare?"

"Why do you say so many nice things about Milton Berle? Are you his brother Frank?"

"Is it a fact that one of the networks has a cleavage censor? And if so, how do you go about getting such a job?"

"Is it true that 'Gunsmoke' is the only Western on tevee which uses live ammunition?"

One reader from Riverside, Calif., enclosed a list of 17 TV commercials with this note: "I find many commercials more imaginative and appealing than many programs. I'd like to see all of these commercials in one show—maybe put together as a Commercial Spectacular. What do you think?"

"I cannot track it down, but didn't one of the Western

stars recently shoot his horse when his gun stuck in his holster?"

"When I go to the movies, Errol Flynn annoys me. What should I do?" (Why not change your seat?)

"Are prison-break TV movies shown in prisons?"

"Who do you think has used up the most ammunition in show business—Olson & Johnson, Jack Webb, Gary Cooper, or Hugh (Wyatt Earp) O'Brian?"

"Has the popularity of old TV movies had an effect on the sale of popcorn?"

❖ ❖ ❖

Most of the foregoing questions were written, I'm reasonably certain, half in earnest, half in jest. The average reader who takes the time and trouble to pen a note to a columnist (assuming he signs his name and address) is an extrovert who likes to see his name in print, a literate person with a fine sense of humor. Such correspondents must not be confused with the people whose unusual acts provide amusing fodder for filler editors, screwball stories that stop you in the middle of a paragraph and make you say to your spouse, "Darling, listen to this one." Many years ago the late newsreel comedian Lew Lehr popularized a catch-phrase that went "Monkeys is the quaziest people." Actually some people make monkeys seem quite normal. To prove our point:

❖ ❖ ❖

Doctors, of course, run into unexpected cases. In Duncan, Oklahoma, a surprised bank teller couldn't understand why she awakened one morning with a rash on her left hand. After countless tests, it was determined that she was allergic to money! In the same cockeyed world of medicine, the Robert Merrills (he's the famed Met Opera baritone) had a nurse who became so attached to their children that she was practically considered a member of the family. She finally had to quit when her medic informed her that a throat malady could be traced to her allergy—children.

❖　❖　❖

Speaking of eating places in Chicago, which we weren't, Irv Kupcinet, the nationally famous *Chicago Sun-Times* columnist, contends there are 34 restaurants in the area all named "Joe's." Doing further research Kups discovered that the owner of the original "Joe's" is named Sam. Following the example of our Chicago friend, we conducted a survey of the New York scene, and turned up 62 restaurants called "Joe's," five of them located between 56th and 60th Streets on Lexington Avenue. The original "Joe's" turned out to be run by a fellow named Irving.

❖　❖　❖

Oddball behavior isn't limited to any locality or nationality. In Mexico City, a movie theater usher, to get even for being fired, threw a pound of pepper into the air-conditioning system. (The jail sentence he received was nothing to sneeze at!)

❖　❖　❖

Once upon a time not too long ago, Bambi, my wife's poodle, was en route to the family farm in Columbia, Conn., along Merritt Parkway, when she suddenly gave birth to a little Bambi. We thought this was unusual and exciting until we learned that in New Jersey there is a Garden State Parkway Stork Club. Members of this limited society are boys and girls who were born on the Parkway while being driven to the nearest maternity hospital.

❖　❖　❖

A friend of ours, Ezra Dolan of *Parade* magazine, was told by his wife's obstetrician that the expected newcomers would be twins. In anticipation of their arrival Ezra and his wife, Vivian, had an announcement prepared reading: "Mr. Mr. and and Mrs. Mrs. Ezra Ezra Dolan Dolan Announce Announce the the birth birth of of twins twins." This would have been one of the most unique of all birth announcements, excepting for one slight miscalculation—the twins turned out to be one very sturdy little boy, now old enough to deny this story!

❖　❖　❖

I don't know where this item came from, but I think, in a way, it's indicative of the times. An applicant for a job in the Cincinnati Department of Sanitation was asked to fill out an application which included the instructions "List all of the positions you've had including your last employer—and work backward." The applicant wrote: *frodnekcez sletoh.* To save you time, this is Zeckendorf Hotels backwards.

❖　❖　❖

A young man out of work read in the Hartford *Courant* that an especially good job was open in Memphis. Being close to broke, the applicant sent a collect telegram to the personnel director of the firm in question, reading: "I'm hitch hiking way to Memphis to accept vacancy. Stop. Please deduct cost of this wire from first week's salary." (Yes—he did get the job!)

❖ ❖ ❖

When a Grand Prairie, Texas, applicant for a position at an aircraft plant was asked if he had any military background and if so to name the dates in service, he wrote: "I have dated some real dolls from Miami Beach, Boston, New York, and Chicago. If further details are required I'll look up my old address book."

❖ ❖ ❖

Another job hunter, seeking a position in Pittsburgh, was stumped when he came to a question in the application form which asked "What machines are you capable of operating?" He wrote in, "Nickel, dime, quarter, and pinball machines."

❖ ❖ ❖

Speaking of jobs, as a stunt the Larry Mathews all-night chain of beauty salons pulled a beaut. They advertised for the homeliest girl in town, then hired the girl to sit in their window with a sign hung around her neck reading "Don't let this happen to you!"

❖ ❖ ❖

Murray Franklin, who runs a laugh factory club in Miami Beach, got tired of having his bartenders drink up all his profits, so he called up columnist Paul Bruun and had him insert an ad in the *Miami Sun* reading: "Wanted: A bartender with ulcers."

❖ ❖ ❖

The housing situation in Hollywood is getting worse day by day, so much so that Dr. Allan Aronson insists a N.Y.

plastic surgeon invaded the movie colony and announced in the *Hollywood Reporter* that he would exchange a new nose for a three-room apartment.

❖   ❖   ❖

Inventions continue to excite and amuse the people in the U.S. Patent Office, through whose hands all inquiries and applications for patents pass. Goofiest in a long time was the invention perfected by a man who was obviously a student of human psychology. He developed a gadget useful only to actors. It is attached to an automobile's four tires. When a flat occurs, instead of hissing, the tire applauds!

❖   ❖   ❖

I don't know whether it's because they're lonesome or restless, but Americans of all ages are champion joiners. Probably the most rabid fraternal group members in the country are the young people who belong to Celebrity Fan clubs. I'd say that between Elvis Presley, Johnny Mathis, Jimmy Dean, Ricky Nelson, Sal Mineo, Julius LaRosa and a half dozen other young singers, particularly rock 'n' roll idols, there are more than 8,000,000 teenage girl and boy members of fan clubs. There used to be a time when the Hollywood stars built up their mail by having their press agents organize fan clubs. But neither movie stars nor the average television celebrities are honored by such adulation these days.

I'll never forget, back in '41, when Frank Sinatra dropped into a Broadway barbershop for a hair trim. Within 20 minutes, hundreds of hero-worshippers tried to crowd their way into the shop—to get a strand of their favorite crooner's curls. "We use the hair as good luck charms," one of the hysterical kids breathlessly explained.

❖   ❖   ❖

During the smallpox scare of some summers ago, a group of folks living in the Bay Ridge district of Brooklyn were all vaccinated by the same nurses. So, naturally, they formed the "Non-Contagious Friendship Club."

But my favorite is the "Flatbush Mothers Thursday Mid-Afternoon Gin-Rummy Club" which meets on Fridays.

When TV first loomed large on the national scene, countless numbers of Television Clubs were organized—members pooling a few dollars each to buy a set—with all dues going to purchase refreshments for those evenings when members got together to witness video entertainment.

Chicagoans may be familiar with the National Good Egg Club. Membership cards identify bearers as "Good Eggs" and the dues consist of eating eggs and getting other good eggs to eat eggs too. Oh, yes. The Poultry and Egg National Board is the sponsor—and as you might suspect, its business is promoting the wider consumption of—ah, ha—eggs.

Sometimes clubs are formed to lobby against what certain folks feel is an unfair practice. In Chickasha, Okla., for example, the bald-headed men of the community organized to force barber shops to only charge half-price for cutting the few remaining hairs of its members.

My nod for a really progressive organization is the one formed by some housewives in a suburb of Boston called the Housewives Anti-Inflation Society. Whenever a member runs across an item she thinks is over-priced, the butcher or baker or dressmaker is handed a card which reads: "No buy. Why? Too high! Goom Bye!"

❖   ❖   ❖

The insurance companies will tell you that there's no way in which they can anticipate strange accidents. Such an example is offered by an adventuresome young gentleman named Tom Front of Oakland, Calif., who made a habit of shaving with a straight razor. While shaving, Tom tried to shoo off a fly with his razor—missed by a few inches, and snipped off his left ear.

❖   ❖   ❖

A pretty young wife of Indianapolis, also had a bathroom accident. She actually dislocated her neck while brushing her teeth. The doctors are still trying to figure it out.

❖   ❖   ❖

And in Montreal a pair of teenagers necking with much too much enthusiasm on a park bench, under the shadow of McGill University, kissed so hard their teeth braces meshed and it was necessary to take them to the University's Clinic where their braces were unbraced (or unembraced?).

❖   ❖   ❖

Here is one that appeared in the Yorkville section of New York that looks like a branch of West Berlin. A couple eating in a Beer Garten decided they would start the feast by ordering oysters. The girl broke a tooth biting into one of the oysters and, with her 20-20 eyesight, noticed that the break was caused by a pearl. The next day she had it appraised and found it to be worth around $200—which broke up a beautiful friendship. Not only did the girl claim ownership of the pearl, but so did the restaurant owner, as well as her date. The impartial judge demonstrated his acumen by awarding the iridescent little jewel to the escort, saying: "Since he paid for the dinner, he certainly is entitled to anything served including a diamond, a ruby, or—a pearl."

❖   ❖   ❖

New York City, which has more parking lots than parking space or housing projects, recently broke into the news when a very penitent young fellow was fined $20 for driving without a license. He admitted he couldn't obtain one because of faulty eyesight. When asked what he did for a living, he said, "I work in a parking lot, parking cars."

❖   ❖   ❖

Incidentally, New York's Chief Magistrate John Murtagh, called recently to confirm a tip-off. It was true, he told me, that many motorists, found guilty of some violations in New York's traffic courts, try to charge the fines on a Diner's Club card.

❖   ❖   ❖

Most people are honest, the original Damon Runyon "Lemon Drop Kid" Swifty Morgan insists, because they're afraid to face the consequences of being dishonest. However, the one area in which so many citizens take great glee in cheating is on their income tax returns. The custom of paying taxes on income was first introduced in Britain back in the year 1799, and the tax collector had to make his door-to-door rounds flanked by two bodyguards. They murdered more tax collectors in those days than mobsters erased rum-runners during the American Error of Prohibition.

Incidentally, while I wasn't around then, I have it on good authority that in ancient Egypt the Treasury was referred to as "The White House." No connection with the Washington establishment, for the occupant there pays taxes just as heavily as we do. As a matter of fact I read the other day where Ike loses about $20,000 a year working for us. He can't do anything about it because a President isn't permitted to have any side-lines such as guesting on panel television shows, lecturing, or giving golf exhibitions at so much a head.

❖   ❖   ❖

Perry Como, along with Bob Hope, Bing Crosby, Arthur Godfrey, Jack Webb, Milton Berle, Joan Crawford, Lucille Ball and other astronomically-high income earners who keep the treasury solvent, send "thank you" notes along with their checks to Uncle Sam.

But perhaps the ultimate in tax frustration was reached by one woman, who won a two-family house on a radio quiz show. Her enthusiasm was dampened when she was told she had to pay the government a tax on her prize. Unable to get up enough cash to meet the assessment, she wrote the Internal Revenue Service saying, "You fellows take the lower floor and let me keep the upper floor of the house." (Guess she kept the basement for state taxes.)

❖   ❖   ❖

That reminds us of the millionaire who died and asked to be cremated. Along with the ashes went a note to the Internal Revenue Service reading: "I thought you'd want these—you've taken practically everything else."

❖   ❖   ❖

One of the oddest deductions claimed on an income tax return—and granted—was reported by the Internal Revenue Commission in Albany, N.Y. It listed as a legitimate business deduction by a grocer an item of $37.62 for food fed to cats to catch mice in the store.

❖　❖　❖

Jack T. Lewis of Litchfield, Minn., added a postscript to his tax return which probably did his heart good. Said Mr. L: "You remind me of cannibals. Do you know how they paid their taxes? When taxes got higher than the cost of living and food—they ate the tax collector."

❖　❖　❖

Washington won't appreciate this, but when a Birmingham newspaper polled citizens to determine who should have priority in Atomic Bomb shelters in case of an emergency, the group to come in last was politicians.

❖　❖　❖

Fred Waring insists this happened near his inn in Shawnee, Pa. A motorcycle cop, who stopped a motorist because he didn't have a tail light was confounded when the driver said: "I'm not concerned about the tail light; what worries me is what happened to my trailer!"

❖　❖　❖

Hal Leroy, one of the all-time great dancers, lives in Maplewood, N.J. He tells us that in nearby Hackensack, when the police captured a burglar who looted the poor boxes of dozens of churches, the miserable fellow gave as his reason: "I was just gettin' even because my prayers weren't answered."

4

Sex Never Takes a Holiday

A GROUP of us were sitting around a table at LaStrada—a fine little Italian restaurant in the Gramercy Park section of New York run by the di Rose brothers, Joe, Frank, and Louis—discussing the speed with which a new joke or humorous incident travels from coast to coast, from country to country. Steve Allen harked back to when telegraphers, between messages, used to keep the tickers hot by passing along quips that passed in the night.

Max Bygraves, the British Danny Kaye, insisted that a joke told at Dave Chasen's in Hollywood at 3 o'clock on a Friday afternoon would be retold in the bar of the Savoy in London at 5 o'clock the same afternoon.

Senator Ed Ford, along with Peter Donald and Harry Hershfield, wanted to make a bet that either of them could tell a new one at a Lambs Club luncheon and hear it retold five times that same night on tevee and radio.

Whatever the method of rocketing rare laughs across thousands of miles of space, professional funnymen agree that nothing, not even bad news, travels as fast as a topical anecdote in the boy-girl category.

The jokes that get the preferred treatment are those with a sex angle. It need not be a smutty joke—preferably a smart one. Sex is a common denominator that goes all the way back to the stone age, where cavemen, it is said, would actually chisel a chuckle into a rock.

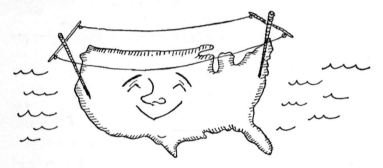

Sex, which used to be a word used only in whispers by our parents when I was a child, is now a family topic of conversation. If you want to know what's going on in the world, don't explain the facts of life to your children. Ask them to explain the facts of life to you. For example, I ran into the 11-year-old daughter of a close friend of ours the other evening, and with nary a howdy-doody, the little doll said, "Uncle Hy, do you know what they call intercourse on the moon?" Slightly abashed I shook my head. "On the moon," she said blandly, "they call it outercourse!"

❖   ❖   ❖

Many schools actually include sex instruction in their curriculum and from what I've been able to gather it has a certain value—the teachers learn quite a bit. This same conclusion must have been reached by the Bridgeport, Conn., Board of Education which voted against sex instruction in classrooms. However they voted to launch a new project —to teach the facts of life to parents.

❖ ❖ ❖

Movies and books (especially the paper-cover variety you pluck from a rack or bail out of a vending machine as you rush for a train or plane) find sales brisk if the titles are lurid and the cover illustrations risque. The same psychological approach applies to record albums. I've seen album covers which were so hot they melted the wax contents. The theory, I suppose, is that the American teenager (this group buys some 65 per cent of the waxworks) is highly impressionable and eagerly goes for an album exposing pornographic art on the cover. I ran into one 17-year-old girl, in covering a teenage story some time ago about the frightening number of high school girls who get pregnant, and discovered her room papered with full-color record album covers. The montage was so startling, the models so scantily clad and provocatively posed, I doubt if Polly Adler in her prime would have permitted the foyer of her bordello to flaunt such slop.

Anyway, back on the track, even lecture bureaus attempt to slant the subjects of speechmakers along sexpot lines. This came about accidentally when a University of Virginia math professor agreed to speak at a women's university on a dull subject called "Convex Sets and Inequalities." He didn't understand until after the lecture why a full house greeted him. Then came the dawn. Some well-meaning clerk misinterpreted the first two words, changing the subject on the bulletin board to read "Convicts, Sex, and Inequalities."

❖   ❖   ❖

And I think the height of something or other was reached when a Boston book store returned an expensive copy of a volume titled "The Handy Manual of Sex" to the publisher with this explanation: "Customer couldn't wait!"

❖   ❖   ❖

Earl Wilson, who fashioned an entire column format on busty gals, saw this sign in a Fifth Avenue dress shop: OUR GOWNS ARE SOUTHERN STYLE—SHOW ENOUGH! And a Bloomington, Ind., newspaper claims that this sign was posted on the bulletin board of the local Veteran's Airport: NOTICE: ABSOLUTELY NO FLYING OVER NUDIST CAMP LOCATED EXACTLY 8 MILES SSW ON TRUE COURSE OF 190°.

❖   ❖   ❖

Jack Entratter, pioneer Las Vegas showman, passes along the information that the stewardesses on the Western Air Lines planes which make routine flights over Wyoming's Grand Teton mountain ranges, used to blush when passengers wanted to know the English meaning of "Grand Tetons." An airline public relations man supplied the stock answer: "Sweater Girl Mountains."

❖   ❖   ❖

Sam Levenson tells about a little boy and girl who ran out of games to play when the lad said, "Let's play pregnant." When asked the rules of the game, the imaginative young man explained, "We go to the bathroom. I'll shave and you get nauseous!"

❖   ❖   ❖

You may recall reading the story out of Los Angeles, Calif., where a flagpole sitter was accused of raping a 19-year-old girl 65 feet atop the pole. He won an acquittal when the court, in general, agreed with public sentiment—that the girl must have known when she climbed up the pole that she wasn't going that far to play tiddly-winks. A defendant in a similar case in El Paso also won his freedom after being accused of raping a 14-year-old girl at the top of a flagpole. Seems the girl made a habit of putting men in awkward positions, then charging them with rape.

❖   ❖   ❖

Along similar lines is an incident Peter Donald recalls having heard when he was doing his twelfth season of emceeing Don McNeil's "Breakfast Club" program. A super-modern young mother who believed in letting her 6-year-old daughter in on all the facts of life, was given cause to pause one day when the two of them boarded a crowded bus. After hanging on to her mother's skirts awhile and studying all the men who were seated as the females stood, the girl shrilly shouted: "Is there nobody on this bus who'll be a gentleman and give my tired pregnant mother a seat?" (The very unpregnant mother shrank to the size of her daughter.)

❖   ❖   ❖

Mike Wardell, an old army friend, recalls the time he was acting as temporary information officer at the WAC center in Ft. Dix, N.J., when a former WAC called to ask if the G.I. Bill of Rights covered hospitalization for maternity. Mike, a little confused, answered: "That depends, sir—I mean madam. Was this a service-incurred disability?"

❖   ❖   ❖

Perfume firms have turned to every possible device to convince prospective buyers that their products are the sexiest. One manufacturer even went so far as to try and name his perfume "Rape," but the ad agency, Better Business Bureau, and a more realistic spouse talked that idea out of the perfumer's head. However, there are shadings to the thought that perfume can make a wolf out of a sheep. In New York a wise and generous furrier frequently permits male customers to borrow mink stoles for dates who cannot afford to own such furs. He cautions the girls, however, not to dab any perfume on their shoulders before pouring on the minks. That the scent sticks to the stole and makes it smell second-hand to the next wearer or possibly the buyer who wishes to own it permanently.

❖   ❖   ❖

Perhaps it's incredible, but in Hartford an insurance firm instructs female employees to use perfume on one ear only, so that male employees won't have to explain the whiff to the wife.

❖   ❖   ❖

Dick Shawn was driving through the Holland Tunnel when he saw a newlyweds' car speed by with old shoes, horseshoes, and so on dangling from the rear bumper together with a sign: "Atlantic City Today—Hot Springs Tonight."

❖   ❖   ❖

Jack Waldron, the comic who discovered Jack E. Leonard in a Chicago cafe and fathered his style of quick-quipping, revisited his hometown recently and saw this sign in a local used furniture store window: LOVE SEAT FOR SALE, $5. OWNER HAS HORRIBLE INFERIORITY COMPLEX.

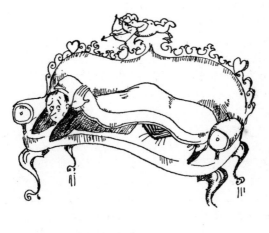

❖   ❖   ❖

And the humor editors of the *Reader's Digest* who pick delicious fillers for the magazine with the greatest circulation in the world, went all the way to Bromsgrove, England, to find this sign: MID-WORCESTERSHIRE CENTRE FOR ARTIFICIAL INSEMINATION. ALL PERSONS ENTERING THESE PREMISES DO SO AT THEIR OWN RISK.

❖   ❖   ❖

One story I like to tell when I have to do an informal lecture about columning concerns an 88-year-old man living in the Midwest. Some time ago I used an item on the radio announcing that this vigorous old timer, then 80 years old, had just become a father. A year later, to the dot, he became a father again—and then again, when he was 85 years old. Upon that occasion I phoned to ask him if he had any secret formula for longevity and virility that I might pass on to my listeners and readers.

"Nope, son," he said, "don't do nothin' unusual. Sit and rock mostly. When I ain't plowin' or pitchin' a little hay."

"Do you take vitamin pills or indulge in any form of exercise?" I asked, anxious to hang my hat on a controversial or educational peg.

"Well, sir," he said, sort of cantankerously, "seems to me about the only thing I do in that neighborhood is something I've been doing since I was a young man. Every morning and every night I chin the bar. I used to chin it 30 times, now I don't overdo it, just chin myself maybe 10 times a day."

I told the story over the air an hour later and, bigosh, within three days I learned that not a single chinning bar was available for sale east of the Rocky Mountains! I know. I tried to buy one myself.

5

Tevee or Not Tevee

I DON'T THINK anything has ever had such a powerful impact on America as television. It's changed eating, sleeping, wooing, and living habits; it's created an era of rudeness, inhospitality, and belligerency; it's made 170,000,000 critics out of fun-loving citizens and converted the average living room into a room where there's no living with the average spouse. Television is a monster that gobbles up time and talent, causes cold suppers, and hot arguments. If interest in the peep-show boxes continues to grow, we'll wind up a nation of squinters. For example, a woman in Indianapolis got a divorce on the grounds that her husband cracked a couple of ribs practicing wrestling holds he saw on TV. Again, Long Island City police were tipped off by a landlady who saw a similar plot on tevee, that one of her boarders was making a hydrogen bomb. Investigation revealed the unsuspecting brunette suspect was siphoning small quantities out of a gallon can of peroxide of hydrogen to keep her hair a natural blonde.

❖   ❖   ❖

Tevee even has a hand deciding marital messes. Bennett Korn, who runs Channel 5 in New York, was asked to supply kinescopes of a wrestling bout as evidence in a divorce suit. The wife discovered her husband, who was supposed to be at work in the office, working over his secretary at the ringside.

❖   ❖   ❖

There's also unintentional humor created by the monster. In Bethpage, L.I., Mrs. Ralph Gardner grew tired of having her daughter Eve and her sons Mike and Richard watch tevee all day and night long. So she got rid of the set and bought a piano. When the piano arrived, Eve said, "Mother, what do we put on the roof to show the neighbors we have a piano?"

❖   ❖   ❖

Television problems are now world-wide. In London, a judge acquitted a young woman of overtime parking charges when she justified the minor violation. "I just had my hair done for a TV commercial shampoo audition," the lady said, "but it was pouring rain and I could not get to my car without ruining my hair and my chances for the job."

❖   ❖   ❖

Educational tevee provides a silver lining. For instance, in Long Beach, Calif., on a recent St. Patrick's Day, a woman actually delivered her own baby without help while watching television from a couch in her living room. Said the new mother with the do-it-yourself-kid, "It was a good movie and I didn't want to turn it off." (Several independent stations incidentally have actually shown the birth of a baby on tevee.)

❖   ❖   ❖

A Dallas tavern makes no bones about not offering tevee to elbow benders. "If you want TV go elsewhere," a notice reads, "but if you stick around you'll see better fights here than on TV."

❖   ❖   ❖

Many clubs maintain TV sets in their bars while patrons wait to be seated. The bar at the Slate Brothers Club in Beverly Hills has a sign over the tevee set: "If this picture looks clear to you, you've had enough to drink."

❖   ❖   ❖

The judiciary is also influenced by the picture medium. A retired circuit court judge near Riverside, Calif., anxious to emulate his counterpart in TV adult westerns, put this ad in the personal columns of a tevee trade paper: "Have gavel. Will travel."

❖   ❖   ❖

Even burglars mix business with pleasure. In Providence, R.I., a thug walked into the kitchen of housewife Beulah Noyes, ordered scrambled eggs, then sat down with her to watch television for three hours—at gunpoint—and walked out leaving a 25¢ tip.

❖   ❖   ❖

And a dude ranch near Poughkeepsie (my old General, Colin MacRae sent this one on to me) caters to potential singing cowboys with this scale of prices: "Riding Lessons, $3.50 per hour; with Guitar, $5."

❖   ❖   ❖

Then there's an antique store on Third Avenue, near Danny's restaurant, which displayed an old 10-inch tevee set in its window with a sign over it reading: "For Sale— Colonial Type Tevee Set, $35."

About two blocks away from the antique dealer, there's a luncheonette calling itself "Ye Olde Tea Shoppe Televisione Snack Bar."

❖   ❖   ❖

Jack Barry, one of the greats of the big money tevee quiz pioneer emcees, actually participated in this unusual exchange of conversation. When, on "Tic Tac Dough" he asked an International Cafe show-girl what a philatelist was, she replied: "A philatelist is a person who believes that whatever is going to happen is going to happen." (Know something funny? It got such a big laugh she walked out a winner.)

❖   ❖   ❖

My friend Fred Dickenson, warden of San Quentin prison, took a survey for us to determine what television shows were favorites with the inmates of his American plan hoosegow. These were the winners: "Man With a Gun," "Have

47

Gun, Will Travel," "Scarface Al Capone," "Gas House Gang," "The Crooked Cop," "Colt 45," and "Gunsmoke."

❖   ❖   ❖

At 4:15 every working day, the thousand or so employees of McCann-Erickson ad agency are treated to a five-minute news broadcast prepared and delivered by a member of the staff. The news is dotted with "commercials" billboarding the tevee or radio shows the agency clients have scheduled for that evening.

❖   ❖   ❖

Walter Slezak took his son Leo to the original Edgar Allan Poe Cottage in the Bronx, now a museum, where both inspected the sparse furnishings. "Mr. Poe," Leo commented, "must have been awfully poor—he didn't even have one television set!"

❖   ❖   ❖

Steve Krantz, a brilliant tevee program creator, also discovered that the medium's influence on young people is staggering. Steve asked the 7-year-old son of a friend of his if he ever watched a baseball game in person. "No," the lad admitted, "but I'd like to. Trouble is I don't know which TV station to write for tickets."

❖   ❖   ❖

To give you an idea of how penetrating is the influence of tevee Westerns on the small fry, this happened in the class of Moss Hart and Kitty Carlisle's young son. All the kids were told that the next day they'd be taught drawing, so please come prepared. Came the following morning and half the class showed up ready for the drawing lesson—they all brought along cap pistols and holsters.

❖   ❖   ❖

Unable to gain possession of the set to watch a favorite program, restaurateur Sid Allen finally discovered a positive way to get rid of the interference on his television set. He sent the children to camp.

❖   ❖   ❖

Tevee has also familiarized youngsters with hospitals. After being permitted to stay up late to watch a heart operation televised, Toots Shor's daughter got to talking about her experiences with surgeons. "I was in hospitals twice," she volunteered. "Once when I was born and once when I had my tonsils taken out. I think I enjoyed being born much more!"

❖   ❖   ❖

I don't think you have any idea of how many of the same corny phrases, better known as clichés, pop up almost every time you turn on TV.

As a matter of record, hundreds of movies use the same words, the same sets, the same horses, the same cowboys, the same pure and unadulterated ranchers' daughters, the same hideouts, the same wagon trains, the same mountains, the same corrals, the same saloons, the same artillery, the same blank bullets, the same familiar everything but the title.

Next to the hoss operas, the whodunits, or private eye films (or those live taped by tevee packagers), stick to the good old tried and true clichés without which villains, gunslingers, cops and detectives, characters on both sides of the law would be speechless. The soap operas, too—those sturdy if weepy willow trees, the great foundation of daytime television—frequently have their romantic but troubled players toss around the same clichés with great and reckless glee.

For some six months we had a group of tevee addicts monitor their sets and jot down some of these clichés. The compilation is fascinating and you'll find most of the following will ring familiar to your ears. Maybe you'll even be inspired to play the cliché game and you might even become a successful script writer in your spare time.

For instance, if you'd like to toss off a story in the private-eye category, a generous sprinkling of the following will make you sound like a professional:

"All our lives we'll be hiding, afraid of every shadow."
"From now on, it's just you and me, Baby."
"Do what you want with me, but let the girl go."
"The boys downtown don't like the way you're running things."
"But I have to report all gun wounds to the police."
"We have ways of making people talk."
"I'll do the thinking for both of us."

"I'm calling you from a phone booth near the antique store; I'm sure I'm being followed."

"I'll ask the questions, mister."

"I'm prepared to make it worth your while."

"Steve, Joe, Lefty, Louie, Mike, Harry—I've got something to say. There's a rat here among us."

"I'm goin' to say goodby, now, but promise me you'll be good to my sister; she's all I got."

"Okay, copper, let's see how tough you are without a gun."

"Damn them, it's tear gas."

"Paul told me you used to be a ganster, Daddy. I gave him a black eye because it's not true—is it?"

If soap opera is more up your alley, here's some sample dialogue that should get you started:

"We live in two different worlds."

"Why didn't you tell me we were going to have a baby?"

"You can't buy my love."

"Please put it away, darling; you've had enough to drink for one evening."

"My husband will be home any minute."

"Your son won first prize in an essay contest. At least you can congratulate him."

"I gave up my stage career and where did it get me?"

"Everybody knows about it but his wife."

"Everybody knows about it but her husband."

"No, darling, I've got to do this my way—alone."

Westerns, of course, are a gold mine of stock phrases, and I'm sometimes convinced that a whole western could be written in which the characters utter nothing but clichés.

Take the following, for instance. Even without arranging them in any special order, they seem to offer a good outline for a fairly taut cowboy-and-Indian drama:

"Ma'am, you can't walk out there in the desert heat without some protection."

"I heard your horse; come in."

"Quick, out the back way!"

"Bartender, serve this hombre a glass of milk."

"It ain't healthy not drinkin' with me, strangerrrr . . ."

"I ain't caught yer name, mistuh." Reply: *"I ain't throwed it yet."*

"That's a mighty fine colt yuh got there."

"Say, what I gotta do ta make ya draw on me?"

"You haven't got the guts to pull that trigger."

"This time the Ringo Kid's gone too far; I'm joinin' your posse."

"Indian chief say white man no talk straight."

"When moon rise over mountain, Blue Coat die."

"If troops don't come soon, I wouldn't give a plugged nickel for our chances."

"Good Lord, Len, how wuz I ta know you wuz the little kid brother I ain't seen since you wuz calf age?"

"It means two or three days of hard ridin', Zeke."

Write your own ending. I personally favor having the whole dang outfit massacred, with a fadeout showing the Injuns riding off into the sunset and shouting gaily, "Let's see how the Great White Father likes *that!*"

Of course, none of the above categories may appeal to you. If not, then here are some hardy clichés on other subjects around which you can build your tale:

"It's your show, kid; go out there and knock 'em dead."

"We's dun it, Miss Lucy, we's dun it; Lady Bell's wun the Derby."

"If this leaks out to the press, we're ruined."

"You say he's a bum. I knew him when he was the greatest fighter in the ring." (A companion piece to this is: *"When I'm gonna get a crack at the title?"*)

"Your tongue is sharp, Sir George. Let us test if your sword be as sharp as your tongue."

"Listen, the drums have stopped. I don't like it; I don't like it one bit."

You think I'm kidding about this tevee cliché stuff? Next time you settle down for an evening of television, keep your ears open; you'll hear at least half a dozen of the immortal phrases printed above.

6

Shop, Look, and Listen

A BROADWAY COLUMNIST has a wonderful time through the years. He meets thousands of important people on an equal footing. Eats and drinks at the finest restaurants, travels all over the country and world. Faces microphones and cameras. And enjoys every hammy second of it! But one of the greatest kicks this one ever got was strictly by coincidence.

I was invited to act as master-of-ceremonies right on the fifth floor of Macy's Department Store in New York, to interview such noted TV luminaries as Garry Moore, Julius La-Rosa, Patti Page, Richard ("Have Gun, Will Travel") Boone, Gene ("Bat Masterson") Barry, Kathryn ("Mrs. Bing") Crosby, Hugh ("Wyatt Earp") O'Brian, Dick Clark, and other famed folks.

The kick didn't come out of the exchange of public conversation, although it was fun, nor from the warm response of the customers who flock to Macy's each year to attend the annual TV and Music Festival. What gave us the big boot (and the store's Miss Kay Vincent will learn this for the first time when she reads this book) was the realization that I finally made it—that I was a big shot at Macy's, right on the same floor where I had demonstrated toy trains after school during two pre-Christmas shopping spells.

Ever since that early chore, I've sort of felt a close kinship to department stores. I even spent some years working as a promotion consultant to the hundreds of clients of Felix Lillienthal & Co., resident buyers, and to Milton Greenbaum of the kingpin outfit, Kirby-Block Company. It's only natural then, that I kept a file of oddities through the years under the heading, "Shop, Look, & Listen." Let's ransack that file.

❖   ❖   ❖

This actually happened in a New York store (not Macy's!) a week before Christmas. It proved that everyone doesn't necessarily imbibe of the Yuletide spirit. One afternoon, surrounded by dozens of screaming, laughing, clawing children, the Santa Claus on toytown duty in the store was approached by a middle-aged woman. The minute he saw her his smile disappeared, his ruddy face went white. It was his wife serving him with desertion papers.

❖   ❖   ❖

There's an old and accepted axiom in the retail trade that a woman will buy anything she doesn't need if she thinks she's getting it at a bargain price. Which was one of the reasons a New Rochelle, N.Y., department store wasn't too surprised to receive a letter, enclosing two single dollar bills and instructing: "Please send $2 worth of something I'd like. I like surprises." (They really surprised her—sent eight quarters.)

❖   ❖   ❖

Another shopping habit that drives shop owners to distraction is the old-age custom of females returning purchases. One store in Peoria, Ill., recently closed its doors for 24 hours to try to find out how it was possible to sell 36 dresses one day and have 39 returned the next day. The answer is an oddity in itself. Three of the dresses were sent back by a shoplifter who complained, anonymously, of course, that the store's size 16s were actually 20s and that they ought to be ashamed of themselves!

❖   ❖   ❖

Men, on the other hand, are the easiest shoppers to satisfy. They merely give the size, quantity, request the price and ask only one favor—wrap it up and let 'em get out as fast as possible. A clerk in the men's haberdashery department of Stern's told me, "I've always been under the impression that every man who comes in to buy anything must be double-parked."

❖   ❖   ❖

To encourage early morning shopping, a store in Johannesburg, Africa, stole an idea from the Groucho Marx quiz show. At some moment, between 9 and 11 a.m. a bell rings—and whatever the customer is paying for at the time, she gets free.

❖   ❖   ❖

Down around the Wall Street area, attorney and World War II hero Robert Rosenthal tells me, there's a tailor who guarantees to make you "Look like an adult Western hero for $110." His "Western" package includes a suit with padded John Wayne shoulders, an elastic cummerbund that gives you a Maverick chest by squeezing-in your tummy, and a pair of shoes that make you taller than any wife Mickey Rooney ever married. For an extra $5 the tailor also gives steady customers a list of 'phone numbers of gals who just happen to like men built like what they think you're built like after being measured for his package.

❖   ❖   ❖

A silly one happened in the furniture department of the Outlet Company in Providence, R.I. After purchasing an antique Louis Fourteenth bed, the customer asked that it be returned in exchange for the next larger sized bed—a Louis Fifteenth!

❖   ❖   ❖

Infant shops also lure customers with package bargains. For instance, a store in the Grand Concourse section of the Bronx offers prospective mothers a deal that's so tempting I wouldn't be a bit surprised if some gals tried to become mothers just so they could take advantage of the package proposition. The purchase of a complete layette, carriage, and crib at a total cost of some $365 also includes the services of a baby sitter for any twelve nights the first 12 months of the infant's life.

❖   ❖   ❖

Lee Graham, who used to merchandise the perfume and cosmetics departments at Russek's on Fifth Avenue, recalls the woman who sued another department store for unusual damages. She claimed she'd been sold a perfume guaranteed to make her seductive. One sniff had the reverse effect upon her boy friend, she said, accounting for her two black eyes.

❖   ❖   ❖

Colorful signs lure many patrons into a Lincoln Road (Miami Beach) lingerie shop. The favorite is: "We Can Girdle Your Globe." (Yes,—but can they put you into orbit?)

❖   ❖   ❖

Jack Sterling, CBS radio's waker-upper chatterbox contributes this one. A Madison, Wis., storekeeper who was robbed three times in three months decided to set a trap. He went about it ingeniously and scientifically, putting his watch, ring, and wallet on top of a table, and then setting up an expensive camera to take a flash of the thieves pulling the act. He slept peacefully until a flash awakened him. Then armed with a pistol, he ran to the front of the store only to discover that not only were the watch, wallet, and ring gone, but so, too, were the crooks—and the camera!

❖ ❖ ❖

Peculiar story, datelined Concord, Calif., told about the operator of a men's clothing store underselling a rival through the simple device of stealing some $3,000 to $5,000 worth of the latter's merchandise and selling it at half price. His "merchandising" scheme worked only too well. Both his victim and a detective went shopping and identified the stolen goods.

❖ ❖ ❖

This brings to mind the bitter rivalry between two store-keepers who used to amuse passersby by changing their window signs every morning. They reached the ultimate when one store flashed a notice saying: IF YOU NEED IT, WE HAVE IT. Whereupon the store across the street retorted: IF WE DON'T HAVE IT, THEN YOU DON'T NEED IT.

❖ ❖ ❖

Many such eye-stoppers help bring in business. A Bronx dress store advertised: MATERNITY DRESSES IN ALL SIZES FROM TEEN-AGE UP TO JUNIOR MISS AND GRANDMA'S SIZE. And the men's sport shop in the Hollywood, Fla., $23,000,000 Diplomat Hotel had this sign over a display of bathing trunks: THE LATEST IN SEAT

COVERS. Then there's the shop in the Beverly Hills Hotel that initiated a topic of conversation with an offering of SUPER-SIZED BATH TOWELS—JUST THE THING TO WEAR WHEN ANSWERING THE TELEPHONE.

❖   ❖   ❖

Speaking of towels, a Miami Beach souvenir shop sells linen imprinted with the names of the Fontainebleau, the Eden Roc, the Waldorf, the Ritz, the Hilton, the Astor, the White House, even Alcatraz. "People like to show off," the shopkeeper explains, "and these imprinted towels and tablecloths make them up to be very nervy and well-traveled." The Alcatraz imprint, he added, is strictly an absorbing conversational piece.

❖   ❖   ❖

Shoppers passing a reducing salon in the Washington Heights section of upper Manhattan no longer pass without grinning at the lispy invitation electrically lit: "ARE YOU THICK AND TIRED OF BEING FAT? THEN COME IN AND LET US TAKE YOUR BREADTH AWAY!" . . .

❖   ❖   ❖

I don't know whether you've ever noticed those sly, *double-entendre* ads developed for Springmaid Sheets. Anyway the success of that campaign has individual store copywriters trying to skirt the censors with similar type ads. One such character got away with one such ad in one edition of a Los Angeles newspaper; then it was lifted out of the paper. The victim—or should we say the aggressor—was a ladies accessory shop advertising a special in myriad-colored

61

hose. The caption read: "Sheeeeeer Nylon Hose created for the height of luxury wear—yet so sturdy many women wear nothing else." As you'd expect, the drawing that accompanied the tricky caption showed a model wearing nothing— nothing, that is, but Sheeeeeer Nylon Hose.

❖　❖　❖

Sex plays an important role in inspiring women to buy various products, whether they're just counter-hopping or shopping for real. Neiman-Marcus, the great Dallas institution, are brilliant merchandisers. Here's an example of one little experiment they conducted to determine which of two names to give to the identical product—sheer-shortie-nighties. One group was displayed under the name of "Saints," the others was labeled "Sinners." Even though the "Sinners" were slightly higher priced they sold four times faster than the "Saints."

❖　❖　❖

An antique store on Third Avenue, a few blocks away from John Bruno's famous Pen & Pencil Restaurant, recently

went out of business and announced it in this fashion:
CRIME DOES NOT PAY. NEITHER DOES THE AN-
TIQUE BUSINESS. SO THE HELL WITH IT! . . .

❖   ❖   ❖

Women's Wear, the fine old trade newspaper in the gar-
ment and retailing field, amused readers some time ago by
relaying a notice to salesmen hanging in the buyers' office
of Gimbel's in Pittsburgh. It reads: "We don't give a damn
how much Macy's bought."

❖   ❖   ❖

Similar appeals to sex consciousness were made in St.
Louis where the cosmetics department of Stix, Baer & Fuller
posted this notice: "Our perfumes will hold your man smell-
bound." I prefer the warning a famous London store gives
femme buyers of a popular scent: "Don't risk wearing this
if you're only bluffing." And in Phoenix a furniture store
gets a little risque right in its front windows. They display
two beds. One has dollar bills strewn all over the sheets. The
other has a male and female dummy in a close embrace.
The sign reads: "Softest beds in town—for love or money!"

❖   ❖   ❖

Then there's the Los Angeles maternity shop whose slogan
is: "We Provide the Accessories After the Fact."

❖   ❖   ❖

Now if we can take a little poetic license and get into
the apocryphal rather than the factual news item, I'd like

to relay a story Lenore Meyer, the lovely wife of Miami Beach Boswell Hank Meyer, enjoys telling.

It concerns a rip-snorting, whiskey sodden Wild Western oil millionaire who went shopping for a shave and stomped into a department store barbershop. Approaching the number one chair barber, the bully shouted: "I want a shave, y'understand, and I'll pay you well for it." With that preliminary sound-off the would-be patron took out a fat roll of bills from his pocket, ripped a thousand dollar banknote off the top, tore it in half and gave one half to the frightened barber.

"This, son," he hissed, "is for you. I'll give you the other half of the tip when you finish shaving me, PROVIDED you don't cut me. If you so much as nick me, instead of getting a thousand dollars," he warned, patting a six shooter in his shoulder holster, "I'll shoot you dead. Yu understand?"

The startled barber turned pale. "Mister," he trembled, "I'm sick. I'd better ask another barber to shave you." The barbers at the other chairs took sick suddenly and en masse and ran for cover. But the shoeshine boy got off his bench and said, "I'll take up your proposition, mister."

The braggart nodded, sat down, the boy lathered him up, shaved him, tossed a hot towel over his face and received both halves of the thousand dollar bill. "Young man," the belligerent patron said, "I want to compliment you. Not only are you a fine barber but you are a man of great courage. Do you realize that if you just nicked me once I'd'a killed you?" The young man smiled. "You wouldn'ta had a chance to shoot me, sir" he said. "Every second as I had my sharp razor gliding over your face I said to myself, Sam, be careful, but if you nick this guy, slit his throat!"

7

You Speak Sign Language?

NEXT TO PUNS I think humorous signs, whether intentional or accidental, offer some of the finest examples of current Americana. They usually tell, in a few words, what jokesters take paragraphs to convey and what cartoonists labor over a drawing board for hours to momentarily tickle your funny bone. To a columnist signs take up many a slack in a column, add a fillup to fillers, are almost sure-fire chucklettes to light the load of weightier words. I've been collecting and reporting such signs for many years, from all the way back to when I did the Broadway column for the old *Brooklyn Eagle* and the Translux "Gag Newsreel" we penned for Hartzell Spence when he was editor of United Features' to the newsreel we ran for Jess Gookin, editor at *Parade*, and for the "Twin Views of the News" radio program we shared for five years with the New York *Daily News* columnist Danton Walker over the Mutual Network. Here are some of my favorites.

❖   ❖   ❖

A New York sign painter who made a specialty of lettering signs for union strikers was picketed by men who wore signs saying THESE SIGNS WERE NOT PAINTED BY THE FIRM WE'RE PICKETING.

❖   ❖   ❖

After the last annual St. Patrick's Day parade a drunk was seen weaving along the middle of the green road marker up and down the middle of Fifth Avenue. When accosted by a cop he looked up innocently and said: "I'm just obeying instructions, sonny. Doesn't that sign say 'Walk on the Green —Not Inbetween' ?"

❖   ❖   ❖

We were strolling over to Joe Marsh's Spindletop restaurant and crossing Broadway with Red Buttons when a traffic officer bawled us out. Pointing to the "WALK—DON'T WALK" electric signs blinking on and off at the corner, he

said: "What's with you two guys? By now don't you know how to read a Teleprompter?"

❖   ❖   ❖

Murray Franklin's club in Miami Beach gets patrons into a mellow mood even before they enter the comedian's boite via signs outside the entrance reading: "THIS PLACE OPENED BY MISTAKE." "IF YOU DON'T SEE WHAT YOU WANT, THIS IS IT." "CUSTOMERS WANTED, NO EXPERIENCE NECESSARY, JUST MONEY." Inside you're greeted with a sign that says: "WELCOME SUCKER, IF YOU DON'T SEE WHAT YOU WANT BY NOW MAYBE IT'S TIME TO GO HOME TO YOUR WIFE." Incidentally, despite the frivolity of the saloon, no one offers Murray a drink. "I'm smart enough to sell the stuff," he explains, "but not stupid enough to drink it."

❖   ❖   ❖

Joe Franklin, the young oldtime tevee show authority, visited a friend living in an exclusive Brooklyn apartment house and reports he saw this sign over the list of tenants: "WARNING. DON'T LEAVE BABY CARRIAGES OR SPORTS CARS IN LOBBY."

❖   ❖   ❖

And I love a sign Mike Gardner hung over the soft-drink fountain he established outside his home in Bethpage, L.I.: "LEMONADE—ALL FLAVORS."

❖   ❖   ❖

Ricky Nelson visited Tin Pan Alley last time he was in New York and says he saw this sign strung onto the door-knob of a Be-bop music firm: "REAL GONE—TO LUNCH."

❖ ❖ ❖

Another doozy in sign language was scribbled in chalk over a brick wall in the New Jersey prison where our confrère, Marie Torre, spent ten days for refusing to reveal the source of a story. It read: "EVERYTHING HERE IS FREE BUT ME!"

❖ ❖ ❖

Our old friend Chin says he saw this sign in a Chinese watch repair shop: "NO TICKEE—NO TOCKEE."

❖ ❖ ❖

And in the same vein, we actually saw this sign in a Philadelphia jeweler's window: "CUCKOO CLOCKS PSYCHO-ANALYZED."

❖ ❖ ❖

A Syracuse cleaning and dyeing establishment, in a rather poor neighborhood, displayed this unusual sign: "WHITE STRIPES REPAINTED ON WORN-OUT PIN-STRIPE SUITS."

❖   ❖   ❖

Shrewdest eye-stopper we ever saw in a gas service station was this one: "TAKE ADVANTAGE OF OUR EASY CREDIT PLAN: 100% DOWN, NOTHING TO PAY EACH MONTH."

❖   ❖   ❖

The Press Box bar along New York's steak row has this precautionary sign above the bar: "IT'S EASIER TO SIT TIGHT THAN WALK TIGHT."

❖   ❖   ❖

And Bloomingdale's had this adorable little sign displayed throughout the store's toy department during the last pre-Christmastime: "NO ONE OVER 18 YEARS OF AGE ADMITTED UNLESS ACCOMPANIED BY A CHILD."

❖   ❖   ❖

Along Route 1, where you're likely to run out of gas or have a flat at an odd hour, there's a sign hung over an independent service station reading: "BUZZ TWICE FOR NIGHT SERVICE. THEN KEEP YOUR SHIRT ON 'TILL I GET MY PANTS ON."

❖   ❖   ❖

In a service station of a different nature, a lingerie store, a big bold sign over a display of bras screams: "WE FIX FLATS."

❖   ❖   ❖

And Larry Mathew's Beauty City has a wall sign in the lobby of the Great Northern Hotel advertising its salon with the phrase: "TEN YEARS OFF FOR CASH."

❖   ❖   ❖

Irving Hoffman, the caricaturist, columnist and world traveler, spotted this room-for-rent sign down in Greenwich Village: "ONE ROOM EFFICIENCY, NO BATH, SUITABLE FOR ARTIST."

❖   ❖   ❖

And a Gypsy fortune-telling tribe, with headquarters in an empty store next to Leone's restaurant on West 48th Street, off Broadway, frankly admits: "WE PREDICT ANYTHING BUT THE WEATHER."

❖   ❖   ❖

Tommy Manville, just for fun, had little cards printed and distributed to various marriage license bureaus reading: "OUT TO LUNCH. THINK IT OVER. I'LL BE BACK IN ONE HOUR."

❖   ❖   ❖

I also like the way a reducing parlor puts it up to potential patrons with the sign: "WHAT HAVE YOU TO LOSE?"

❖   ❖   ❖

Max Asnas, the sage of the Stage delicatessen, where the lox and the bagels mix with tux, evening gowns and television stars, sums up his stock-in-trade thisaway: "IF IT SMELLS GOOD WE'VE GOT IT."

❖   ❖   ❖

Barney Greengrass, who caters to the same trade as Mr. Asnas, but on the fish and dairy side, frequently receives wires and telephone calls to ship herrings and other spoilable delicacies across the continent or across the ocean. All such packages are packed in dry ice but still carry the precautionary notice: "IF NOT DELIVERED IN 72 HOURS NEVER MIND DELIVERING AT ALL."

❖   ❖   ❖

Jerry Freeman, right hand man to Marine Colonel Ralph Horgan, the popular Broadway Ford-Mercury-Lincoln dealer, took an old sports car in trade and with one glib sign sold it within 20 minutes. The sign? "MG CODDLED BY OWNER. ONLY $2,399, INCLUDING CARRYING CASE."

❖   ❖   ❖

Speaking of signs that punch time clocks, a one-man department store operator in Hartford, made as certain as possible that he didn't lose any customers when he closed the shop for lunch. His sign read: "BACK IN 30 MINUTES. ALREADY GONE 20."

71

❖   ❖   ❖

Another dry goods shop advertised "BATH TOWELS FOR THE HOLE DAMP FAMILY."

❖   ❖   ❖

This is the kind of sign which could get you killed if you tried to palm it off as a pun without relation to a collection. It was pasted in the hole-in-wall window of a subway lunch-room: "FOR SALE. DOUGHNUT SHOP. OWNER IN A HOLE!"

❖   ❖   ❖

The Vic Tanny influence on reducing inspired a stream of saucy signs in smaller reducing salons coast-to-coast. In Chicago: "DON'T GIVE UP THE SHAPE." In London: "WE ARE EXPERTS IN DEVALUING THE POUND." In a Miami corset shop: "LINE TAMERS." In a Hollywood bra shop: "INFLATION AT PRE-WAR PRICES." In a men's clothing store, a stone's throw from the Yale campus in New Haven, Conn.: "OUR TWEEDS WILL MAKE YOU LOOK LIKE A REAL TWEEDHEART."

❖   ❖   ❖

Frank Farrell notes that even off-beat types of business firms go in for *double-entendre* signs. Like the building sand-blaster who advertised: "CALL US IF YOU HAVE ANY DIRTY STORIES."

❖   ❖   ❖

A Coney Island lunch counter, thriving on the overflow from the King of the Franks, Nathan's, boldly displays this electrically lit sign: "OUR HAMBURGERS ARE MADE— NOT ACCUMULATED."

❖   ❖   ❖

This, I think, must be Bernie Miller's favorite sign because he sent me at least three memos repeating it. It concerns a Houston plumber named Carr who uses this slogan: "HONEST CARR, THE USED JOHN DEALER."

❖   ❖   ❖

My friend, the Rev. Jerry Cacopardo, saw this sign in front of a Ft. Pierce, Fla., church and now uses it on the bulletin board of his own church near Ft. Lauderdale: "NOTICE TO ALL CONCERNED: WE ARE NOW OPEN BETWEEN EASTER AND CHRISTMAS."

❖   ❖   ❖

Here's one we forgot to include in our grouping of reducing salon come-ons, a clever invite issued by a Roanoke, Va., dancing school: "WE GUARANTEE TO CURE YOU OF BEING A WALLFLOWER AND, AT NO EXTRA CHARGE, WILL REMOVE THE POT."

❖   ❖   ❖

Maybe it's just a coincidence, but when the boys began to hang signs in the state capitol building at Harrisburg, Pa., they hung the sign "BIRTH CERTIFICATES" right below the "DEPARTMENT OF LABOR AND INDUSTRY."

❖   ❖   ❖

One sign that never came into being was one suggested to the executives of Seagram by one of their most loyal patrons, Joe E. Lewis. Joe suggested that the distiller's new Park Avenue building entrance should carry a notice reading: "PLEASE REVOLVE USING DOORS."

73

❖   ❖   ❖

Another old favorite is seen constantly in bake shops all over the English-speaking world.

CHOCOLATE CAKES 66¢
99¢ CAKES DOWN UPSIDE

❖   ❖   ❖

Leonard Lyons' column printed a classic about the sign language of another era—the days when Indians sent messages by smoke signals. This one involved a Las Vegas Indian who got impatient waiting for an answer to one of his messages when suddenly the Army dropped a hydrogen bomb and fire and smoke mushroomed skyward. Blinking his eyes the Indian sent back a personal message. "Okeh, okeh," the smoke signal flashed, "I'm sorry I was impatient—but do you have to holler?"

❖   ❖   ❖

And for a lagniappe, before revolving on to the next chapter, we'd like to mention that a N.Y. restaurant named Gatsby's (after the late F. Scott Fitzgerald's *The Great Gatsby*) has this slogan on all printed matter: "You've Read the Book—Now See the Saloon."

74

8

Thugs, Lugs, Mugs, etc.

I GUESS I never stopped being a police buff. And I think you'd share my admiration and respect for the average American cop also if you saw the boys in action against desperate, dope-crazed and lethally armed muggers, hold-up men, or gangsters. Every time a cop puts on his uniform he makes himself a target for every uncaged punk, pervert and potential plunderer. For my money the cop in your town is America's Unknown Hero, the most underpaid and abused of all public servants.

Oddly enough, I've cashed in some of my best stories, real factual whodunits sometimes, by being in the company of detectives, either on active duty, retired, or momentarily relaxed. And the surprising thing I have found out is that many of these veteran officers have established a camaraderie with itinerant lawbreakers, especially those they've collared and helped to haul into the hoosegow. "I just ran into Blinky," one pickpocket squad sergeant mentioned to a couple of his old pals as we were having a late snack at

Lindy's. "How is the old goof?" another plainclothesman asked, almost in affectionate tone.

"What's the bit with the nostalgia about these bums?" I inquired. "It isn't nostalgia," the sergeant grinned, "it's just that you feel sorry for these characters after they've spent half their lives or more behind bars. Some are real bright, in their own way, and excepting for a quirk in their minds would have made good in a legitimate enterprise. When we make a pinch we do so because that's our job. We have no personal animosity unless they get nasty and try to pull a knife or gun on us. Then it's every man for himself.

"Certain categories of criminals are pretty harmless. Like pickpockets or check hikers or con men. Being assigned to such branches of the business, it's amazing how many times you come in contact with the same lawbreakers over the years. This establishes a certain rapport that works both ways. We're not mad with them. They're not mad with us. One fellow I picked up last week for the fourth time on a pickpocketing rap asked if I could hang a charge of manslaughter on him—that he'd draw a lighter sentence in that category than as a Baumes Law fourth offender in his own specialty, pickpocketing. By the third or fourth arrest the jailbird on parole is a pretty shrewd amateur lawyer and can teach a few lawyers a few tricks."

❖ ❖ ❖

I became quite friendly with Warden Fred Dickenson of San Quentin Prison and his predecessor, Warden Clinton T. Duffy, author of "The San Quentin Story," later made into a movie. And whenever we get a chance to sit around a table at Leone's little Italian restaurant (by little I mean it isn't quite as large as Yankee Stadium) both men let fly with quips and anecdotes about men behind bars that make for charming and highly amusing conversation.

It was Fred, for example, who spun a yarn that deserved a full column. Owing to a lot of news items we had to jam into the space that particular day, we trimmed the incident down to a paragraph, and I think we'll do likewise here. The situation revolved around a man who was condemned to hang for murder. A crowd of witnesses had gathered to watch the execution when the warden informed the fellow that the law permitted him to say anything he pleased for ten minutes. When he turned down the invitation to make a speech there was momentary silence; then a witness in the rear spoke up and said "I'll fill in the ten minutes and make a speech, if you'd like." "And exactly who are you?" the warden inquired. The volunteer indentified himself as a politician running for Congress. Whereupon the law official asked the condemned man if he had any objection to such a speech being made. "It's okay with me," the man on the scaffold said, "but, Warden, I wish you'd do me one favor before the Congressman speaks—hang me first!"

❖   ❖   ❖

Some of my favorite little items in the news, on the subject of cops and robbers, are so bizarre you may think I'm pulling your leg. But I'm not. I pass them on exactly as they were reported.

For instance, in New York a police car was stolen while the two radio cops were investigating the theft of a private car. Two days later they found the stolen car right in front of a Bronx precinct with a note attached to the steering wheel reading "Better tighten your brakes. They're dangerous."

❖   ❖   ❖

In Cleveland, Ohio, U.S. Post Office detectives (they're another great, unsung group) took some five years to catch up with a female who made a practice of cashing stolen checks—and getting away with it. The reason the inspectors claimed they had such a difficult time identifying the female thief is understandable, and picturesque. Whenever she approached a male post office teller she wore such a low-cut dress not one of the victims could describe her face.

THUGS, LUGS, MUGS, ETC.

❖ ❖ ❖

Also in the nude news, via UPI, dateline East Los Angeles, was a woman who thought for herself. When picked up in a local bar for wearing nothing but a bra, she shrugged and said: "My roommate wanted her clothes back so I gave them to her."

❖ ❖ ❖

In Wichita, a young man was picked up by police for turning in a false fire alarm, barging into a radio studio, shooting an announcer and, at pistol point, demanding an engineer record his strange conduct. His explanation? "How else could I emphasize how unfair the State Police were in refusing to give me a permit to carry a pistol?"

❖ ❖ ❖

You've read where policemen have helped to deliver babies, save drowning men by blowing air back into their lungs and carrying a 400-pound woman down a fire-escape as the flames licked at her body? Well, one of the strangest cases involving cops coming to the rescue occurred in Plymouth, England, when a harassed matron summoned police to help her unzip a new evening gown when the zipper stuck.

❖ ❖ ❖

Speaking of odd ones, not too long ago the manager of a Scranton hotel reported a theft to police. Someone stole the second floor fire escape!

❖ ❖ ❖

The jailer at the Omaha County Jail received a letter addressed to an inmate who was still on his way to the prison from the court in which he'd been convicted. On the back of the envelope was a notation: "If not in jail yet, please hold for arrival!"

❖   ❖   ❖

And in a San Antonio jail, certain unhep inmates complained bitterly that cha-cha music from the jukebox of an adjoining saloon kept them from enjoying a decent night's sleep.

❖   ❖   ❖

This wasn't exactly walled off, but in a cell especially reserved for drunks to sleep off a bender, the warden of a Bellingham, Wash., prison used his imagination. He had the walls of the alcoholic detention cells painted with colorful cartoons of pink elephants, green snakes, and leopards whose spots changed every now and then.

❖   ❖   ❖

Oh, yes, I almost forgot this one, out of Salt Lake City. The boys running the Utah State Prison's newspaper happily reported the escape of its managing editor with this headline, worthy of Abel Green's *Variety:* "Editor in Chief Now Editor at Large."

❖   ❖   ❖

Which reminds us. The newspaper published at Alcatraz has an amusing masthead motto. It reads: "Alcatraz: The pen with a lifetime guarantee."

And just for the record, there are no less than 29 prisons in the country who refer to their hoosegows as "The Walled-Off Astoria."

❖   ❖   ❖

In Niagara Falls, (and we checked this one carefully because it sounded too pat to be true) the manager of the Bell Aircraft firm showed off a communication he received from an optimistic convict asking the cost of a helicopter and adding "Will it carry two people?" The letter was forwarded to the warden of the Illinois State prison from whence the uplifting inquiry had come.

❖   ❖   ❖

Oldtimers at a famous New York hotel still insist this incident actually happened. It was 3 a.m. Only the room clerk, the night cashier, a relief elevator operator, and a burly house detective were on duty in the deserted lobby. Suddenly four men, dressed in work clothes, strolled in. "I guess this is the carpet, Joe," a member of the foursome, obviously the leader, said. "Would you mind stepping aside, bud?" he smiled at the detective, "we've got work to do." The house dick sleepily stepped aside and walked onto the marble part of the floor while the four strangers rolled up the thick wool carpeting, bound it with wire, cordially extended their thanks and carried the carpet to a truck parked outside reading "Hotel Cleaners." Not until the next morning, when the hotel's manager reported for work and was stunned by the bare floor, did the detective and his associates realize they were witnesses to the theft of a $10,000 carpet.

❖ ❖ ❖

Frank Kridel, who runs the Astor, the Manhattan, and other hotels for the Zeckendorf chain, tells me that petty thievery takes a toll that runs into more than $20,000,000 a year. Much of this, Frank points out, can be charged to otherwise honest, law-abiding citizens. Honeymooners, the Wilton Hotel in Long Beach, Calif., reports, are the worst offenders. They take anything that isn't nailed down, under the head of mementos. Conventioneers run the honeymooners a close second. But they tend to be destructive, not cute or cunning. The Claypool Hotel in Indianapolis used to have so many pictures stolen from its walls that it now hangs prints which are too large to fit into a suitcase. New York's Henry Hudson Hotel, back in the days when John Paul Stack of the Beverly ran the place, once prosecuted a dishonest guest for stealing a coin-operated radio. There is no record, yet, of television sets being stolen from rooms. I suppose the would-be pilferers are frightened by TV's private eyes.

❖ ❖ ❖

In Detroit, florist Carl Keller was held up at gunpoint. By request he gave the stickupman $115 and his business card. "I'd like to return this money when I get a job again," the nervous robber explained.

❖ ❖ ❖

A London thief, caught in the act of lifting a purse, was so angry with himself by the time he filled out the usual form at headquarters that he added the cryptic letters "ABC" after his name. Asked to interpret, he wrote "Absolutely Blooming Careless."

❖   ❖   ❖

In Los Angeles, a thief broke into a diner, prepared a meal for himself, and left a 10-cent tip. "I'd leave a quarter," he wrote, "but the steak was tough."

❖   ❖   ❖

In Pittsburgh, Buddy Hackett wishes to note, a forger committed suicide after spending three months forging a check only to have the bank return it stamped: "Insufficient Funds."

❖   ❖   ❖

And, even in news items, you'll occasionally notice a bored editor slip in a pun. Example: Russ Stewart of the *Chicago Sun-Times* kidded Irv Kupcinet about the man and wife, who according to Kup's column, were arrested for robbing a china shop. Russ summed up the item by commenting: "She washes them—he swipes them."

❖   ❖   ❖

The Bell Telephone Company of Cleveland asked local police to help trace the wisenheimers who were stuffing up the coin slot of a pay telephone and emptying out the jackpots. Nothing unusual about the incident excepting this: the don't-pay station happened to be attached to the lobby wall of the central police station.

❖   ❖   ❖

In case you're not convinced that there's a little ham in every one, even a thief, get an eyeful of this item out of Amarillo. After making good his escape from the local jail, the fugitive had the audacity to telephone a broadcasting station and complain that in all their bulletins seeking his capture they kept mispronouncing his name.

❖   ❖   ❖

Guess I love this one better than most. The burglar who ran loose in Milwaukee by masking his face with an infant's diaper, then robbing the Bottoms Up Tavern.

❖   ❖   ❖

And in Leavenworth, every once in a while the keepers have to feed tranquilizers to a counterfeiter doing 30 years. He breaks down every time he recalls the one big mistake that caught him with his printing plants down. He counterfeited a counterfeit from a counterfeit.

❖   ❖   ❖

And in Newark, the Gross Laboratories reported the theft of 1,500 false teeth. (I guess they were held up by gum-men.)

❖   ❖   ❖

Even the men who inhabit the prisons in Texas think big. A fellow serving a 19-year term for forgery in a Dallas jail also managed to forge his prison records and give himself an extra 3 years, 2 months, and 16 days off for good behavior.

9

Who's Zoo?

EDITORS AND COLUMNISTS discovered long ago that the quickest way to arouse readers from their lethargy and get them to write fan or pan mail is by printing an item about a pet, a baby, or an idol like Elvis Presley. Consequently you'll seldom leaf your way through a newspaper without finding at least one filler story concerning a dog who saved a child, a child who saved a dog, or a man who went to the dogs and thus improved his position in life. Here are some nominations from our scrapbook marked "Who's Zoo."

❖   ❖   ❖

There's an old English law that permits a dog to have two bites on the house before he must be handed over to the authorities for biting off more than the law permits him to chew. Mailmen, in many cities, have an index card showing which pups, in their particular routes, are troublesome, friendly, or moody. Some go so far as to pacify the ornery

87

dogs by rubbing a little meat gravy on an envelope and handing the mail directly to the four-legged master of the house. Bob Christenberry, New York's Postmaster, refers to such precautionary measures as "First Class—five scents due." In Batavia, N.Y., the water department meter inspectors, harassed by barking if not biting dogs, asked the help of postmen, and since using the index system have emerged unscathed from their hazardous calls.

❖   ❖   ❖

A special police squad, raiding a Harlem bottle club recently, thought they were seeing things when a little white poodle raised the roof with his shrill barks. What surprised the cops was seeing the dog wearing a mink jacket and a diamond-studded collar.

❖   ❖   ❖

Jim Bishop, one of my favorite all-time columnists and friends, once had a dog named Duke who was weaned on beer. When forced to become a member in good staggering of Alcoholics Anonymutts, the former imbiber got so disconsolate he actually ran away from home.

A similarly bejeweled and befurred dog, this one a full-sized Great Dane, was seized along with other occupants of a raided apartment by Federal men on the hunt for a dope ring in Chicago. While the two-footed prisoners were found to be clean, an investigator frisked the dog and found some $10,000 worth of heroin concealed in his expensive collar and packs of marijuana cigarettes tucked in the lining of his mink "coat."

❖ ❖ ❖

When we spent some time at Ft. Dix, we met the acquaintance of a collie, belonging to a family in nearby Pemberton, N.J., who refused to take his necessary constitutionals during daylight hours. He preferred to slink out after dark—but not until his master strapped a portable flashlight to a shoulder holster especially tailored for the purpose.

❖ ❖ ❖

Many people think it's smart to feed their pets booze and then watch them walk in a drunken daze. Actually this is frowned upon by the American Society for Prevention of Cruelty to Animals, which says it isn't healthy for a dog to partake of alcohol, that it deadens his nerves and shortens his life. Just about the only thing you can say in favor of this nitwit practice is that you never heard of a dog being arrested as a drunken driver. He, at least, has the good sense to lie down in a corner until the dizzy feeling wears off.

❖   ❖   ❖

A Cleveland matron, busy watching Bat Masterson's latest escapade on tevee, heard her dog crunching on what she thought was a chicken bone. It startled her for a moment, because they had pork and beans for supper with no bones to show for it. During the commercial she checked the source of the crunching and discovered her dog was licking his chops over her chops—a brand new set of dental plates.

❖   ❖   ❖

The Edwin Weilers of Forest Hills, N.Y., have a cocker with a magnetized collar. Not for purposes of decoration but for utilitarian reasons. Every morning the dog creeps under the furniture and comes up with whatever bobby pins, collar buttons, and other metal doodads that might have carelessly dropped the night before.

❖   ❖   ❖

Ofttimes the shoe is on the other foot. Take Will Elkton of Portland, Ore. Convinced that a neighbor wouldn't do anything to stop his dog from yapping all night (and you couldn't blame the dog because he was locked up), Will took retaliatory measures. Having no dog he did the next best thing. On three successive nights he crawled on all fours beneath his neighbor's window and barked and barked 'till he got hoarse.

❖   ❖   ❖

Many dogs have been involved in court cases, frequently on trumped-up charges to get the owners to settle for a few dollars out of court. Down in Raleigh, a dog owner, so nettled at a neighbor's constantly reporting her dog's behavior to the police, turned the tables. Instead of putting a muzzle on her dog, as ordered, she invaded the neighbor's house and at rifle-point slapped the muzzle over his mouth. This resulted in a fine of $10 plus three days in the hoosegow. "But," the contented woman said to reporters, "it's worth it, and I'll do it again when I get out."

❖   ❖   ❖

I remember when we subleased a lovely townhouse one summer directly next door to a vocal coach who believed the fresh air was better than air-conditioning and who kept all his windows open wide while his students screeched. We tried playing the radio at full volume, placed a loud-speaker next to his window, tried in every imaginable way to make him shut his window. But he refused until I got a sudden notion. I decided to let my poodle Lani settle the issue for me. I bought Lan one of those noiseless whistles that can only be heard by dogs and taught him to bark out his brains whenever I blew it. This, in itself, wouldn't have been effective. What stopped my vocal coach neighbor cold in his tracks and forced him to either shut his windows or change his occupation was that whenever I blew the whistle not only did Lani set up a howl but all his friends in the area joined in the general whoop-up.

There's a p.s. to this story. One evening, many years later, we had the famous opera singer, Patrice Munsel, on our TV show. "It's a funny thing," she said when we brought up the incident of the dog whistle, "but to prove what a small world this is, I was one of the students who heard all that barking and wondered what it was all about. I was taking singing lessons from your neighbor that summer."

❖   ❖   ❖

Here's one from out of *Time* magazine. A Chicago woman named Dolores McCrossen lost her dog and asked the police to please try and find him. For identification the cops were told to look for a dachsund wearing red nail polish on its toenails.

❖   ❖   ❖

Some service stations across the nation, realizing that when a dog has to go he has to go just like people, have little comfort stations set aside for the pets of motorists who stop to gas up at their stations. One such thoughful person, near

Willimantic, Conn., actually built a little dog village on the premises. It contains a dog house, a snackery with biscuits, water, and meaty bones, an old fire hydrant, a group of miniature trees and grass patches, and mounds of dirt, all temptingly dog-scented.

❖ ❖ ❖

Also in Chicago, a dog owner was hailed into court for permitting his spaniel to run around without a leash. "I had to," he defended himself and the dog. "Her condition requires plenty of exercise. She's expecting pups."

❖ ❖ ❖

Another chap, Joey Bishop reports from Boston, was speeding along in his open sports car when a motorcycle cop pulled alongside and said "Where you going, to a fire?" "Not exactly," the driver admitted, "but my dog's in heat and the breeze cools her off."

❖ ❖ ❖

Cutest sign we spotted in a long while, though we never could figure out its significance, was one hung in front of a Newark kennel reading "Second Hand Dogs for Sale."

❖ ❖ ❖

Then there's the dog thief who, upon being picked up in Wilmington, Del., on a charge of pupnapping, pleaded innocence. "I don't know whether you know it or not," he told the judge, "but I'd like to remind you that the law says that dogs have no value. And since they haven't any value, I didn't steal anything." The judge, who understood the law better than the thief, admitted the scoundrel was right. However, he tossed him into the clink for ten days anyway, on a charge of stealing the dog's collar!

❖　❖　❖

To get away from dogs and on to other pets for a page or two, let's get to an interesting court case in England. It seems the customs collector classifies imported monkeys as two-footed animals. An importer objected to this classification and took the case to court because there is a smaller import duty on four-footed animals. The judge, a real diplomat, skirted the question neatly. He ruled that monkeys have no feet at all—they have four hands.

❖　❖　❖

Another sign that deserves more circulation. This one in a Los Angeles pet shop window, hung over an empty cage: "Love Birds for Adoption—After They Return from Their Honeymoon."

❖　❖　❖

Glen Cove, N.Y., had itself an oddity worthy of the late Mr. Ripley. A chicken farmer reported a hen straining for three days, then laying a 16-ounce egg, taking one look at it, and falling over dead.

❖　❖　❖

Back home in Columbia, Conn., a local couple, afraid of no animals, became alarmed when they sniffed a skunk in the cellar. Asking a dog catcher for suggestions on how to trap the skunk without trapping themselves, Ben was told to take a loaf of bread, make a trail of crumbs from the basement to the yard, then wait with his shotgun for the skunk to follow the trail outside. The farmer followed instructions, then called his friend back to say he did what he told him, but now there were two skunks in his cellar!

❖   ❖   ❖

And if you don't think livestock has instinct, listen to this tale from a township in Indiana. Jack M. was merrily driving along in his car when it was gored by a bull! Jack's occupation? He's the official artificial inseminator for the county!

❖   ❖   ❖

We'll wind up this round-up with a classified ad in the *Detroit News* that will touch the hearts of all animal lovers. Under the "Wanted" column, the message read: "Wanted: a home for a 7-weeks-old puppy, house broken except when very happy."

10

The Long Cold War Between the Sexes

WE ONCE HAD an army camp commander who signed an order forbidding liquor, women, or dogs on the post. "This order," he stated informally in a postscript handwritten beneath the official pronouncement, "is official but impersonal. I've been in the army for some thirty-five years. I've been to posts all over America and in nine foreign countries and I've yet to see a camp in which you didn't hear an occasional dog barking, a soldier weaving, or a prostitute hiding. Nevertheless orders are orders and this, men, is an order."

❖   ❖   ❖

Of all the entertaining news fillers you see in the daily newspapers, those which have something to do with liquor, dogs, courtship, marriage, and divorce are the most numerous. I've re-read my file of such morsels and herewith pass along to you those which I consider worthy of taking you away from your tevee set for a chapter. We'll start with the war of chemistry between the sexes.

❖   ❖   ❖

Louis Sobol, one of the best liked and respected of the pioneer cream of the crop of Broadway columnists, ran into a well known author who needed the money and signed to write for television. Waving the lucrative contract at his wife he shouted: "See this? It means I'll now be seen in every bar, grill, saloon, and lounge in New York!" His wife just shrugged. "What makes you think," she said icily, "that you haven't been?"

❖   ❖   ❖

In Springfield, Ill., a distraught wife filed for divorce from her husband Harry, a weather forecaster, claiming he was "cold and indifferent." Harry countered with the statement: "We've got nine children already and a tenth is on the way. If this is being cold, I'd better find a new kind of job."

❖   ❖   ❖

Oldest such item in our memory was the Brooklyn woman who sued for divorce claiming her husband spoke to her only eleven times in eleven years. She won the custody of the eleven children.

❖   ❖   ❖

In the hillbilly section of Tennessee a father of 31 children said he was unhappily wed and wanted a divorce. When the judge asked why, if he was so unhappy, he sired so many children, the virile father answered, "I thought maybe, judge, that with that many kids I could lose my wife in the crowd." (The judge decided the father was hanging around with the right crowd and ordered him to continue to do so.)

❖ ❖ ❖

This was like a breath of fresh air compared to the Atlanta husband who sued his wife for divorce claiming she was carrying on a correspondence romance with the neighborhood garbage collector. As evidence he offered 19 love letters he claimed he picked out of the lovers' improvised mailbox— the garbage can.

❖ ❖ ❖

Time magazine reprinted the story of a Pennsylvania woman who had trouble getting a divorce. Her complaint was that her husband, who used to beat her regularly every Christmas, lately started also to beat her on other holidays. (Wonder what he gave her for Mother's Day?)

❖ ❖ ❖

In Detroit, an enterprising girl, who'd been married to five different husbands, recently remarried her first husband. To reporters, the sheepish groom explained, "I guess it musta been my turn again."

❖ ❖ ❖

This one is hard to swallow, but it ran in a reputable Providence, R.I., newspaper. In granting a pre-divorce decree to a local resident, the court insisted that the woman permit her husband to come home once a week to take a bath.

❖ ❖ ❖

In Reno, a long-suffering groom asked for a legal parting because every time he wanted to take a walk without his wife he found his shoes nailed to the closet floor.

❖ ❖ ❖

In Frankfurt, Germany, a bride was awarded a divorce decree when she proved that her husband, a tailor, cut the hems off all her daintiest negligees, then sewed them into bras for the sweetheart he was wooing.

❖ ❖ ❖

A Baltimore woman, asked what reason she had for wanting a divorce from her husband, said she thought he was a liar. "Why just last week," she told the court, "he came into the kitchen wearing his tuxedo and said 'Darling, I'll be back the day after tomorrow. I'm going fishing with the boys."

❖ ❖ ❖

A Memphis woman insisted her husband lost his respect for her. "Whenever we got into an argument he threw a chair at me," she tearfully told the judge. ("She ought to be glad," an eavesdropper whispered, "that it wasn't a love seat.")

❖ ❖ ❖

I don't know where Saul Miller dug up this one, but it sounds like it happens every day. A Miami woman demanded a divorce on the grounds that whenever he was broke her husband tried to exchange her for a new convertible car.

❖   ❖   ❖

Steve Allen swears he saw this sign in a Las Vegas detective agency: "You get the girl. We'll tell you if she's all yours!"

❖   ❖   ❖

After Eddie Fisher and Elizabeth Taylor married in Las Vegas and flew to New York en route to a honeymoon in Spain, some wag hung a sign on the rear bumper of their Carey Cadillac reading "Just Married. Amateur Night."

❖   ❖   ❖

A Reno preacher makes photostats of all licenses issued to couples he marries, then mails copies to mark every anniversary. He usually receives thank you notes, but in one instance he received a nasty wire saying: "Dear Preacher: Wish you wouldn't be so thoughtful. The one you married me to was a dud and I hate to be reminded I ever knew her."

❖   ❖   ❖

In Cincinnati, a 75-year-old matron registered for a secretarial course. Asked why, at that age, she wished to launch a new career, she cackled, "Career my eye, I just want to be able to read my late husband's diary. He kept it in shorthand."

❖   ❖   ❖

If you've got time, figure this one out and explain it to me. In Brockenhurst, England, 63-year-old composer William Macky announced his intention of marrying a pretty young music teacher 42 years his junior. "The marriage," the dispatch said, "will make my fiancé her own aunt, her father's sister-in-law, and her brothers' aunt. (And I always thought when a girl married she became a bride!)

❖   ❖   ❖

In Syracuse, my friend Rev. Ralph Philbrook, Chaplain of the Auburn State Prison, reports, a young man, watching a doctor take three stitches out of his fiancee's head, fainted, hit his head on a marble floor, and had to have twelve stitches taken in his own scalp. No, the vicious cycle didn't continue; the bride-to-be didn't faint.

❖   ❖   ❖

In Sand Lake, Mich., a new groom suddenly realized that he forgot to give his new bride the customary good morning kiss as he left for work. He turned his car around and collided with his wife who was rushing to overtake him for the same sentimental reason.

❖ ❖ ❖

An indiscriminate Boston ventriloquist was upbraided by the magistrate for deserting his wife and told he must grow up and choose between his wife and his dummy. So he chose the dummy.

❖ ❖ ❖

These few lines might provide a great source of pleasure if you subtly suggest your wife read them aloud. Martha W. Griffiths, a judge at the Detroit Recorder's Court, recently ruled that it is not a crime for a husband to get angry at a wife who refuses to scrub his back.

❖ ❖ ❖

Right in Little Old New York, public relations genius Sandy Pitofsky resigned as executive director of the Bachelor's Club for the simple reason that he intended taking out a marriage license. (Incidentally, if you saw his beautiful bride, you could understand what motivated him into breaking up the club.)

❖ ❖ ❖

A fellow charged with bigamy in a Florida court shrugged off the indictment. "I'd do it again, and again, and again," he said. "It just so happens I don't believe in divorce."

❖ ❖ ❖

Here's one I used many years ago, and, if I'm not mistaken, it was reprinted by most of the pocket-sized magazines. It referred to a Chicago domestic relations judge who had a sticky problem. Seems a divorcee tried to get the court to restrain her ex-husband from remitting his monthly alimony in dollar bills stuck together in a bunch of partly licked lollipops. "So what," the vituperative ex-hubby shrugged, "it's sucker money, ain't it?"

❖   ❖   ❖

Then there's the young lady, who, after she broke her engagement, returned all her frustrated suitor's letters marked "Fourth Class Male."

❖   ❖   ❖

In Denver, a certain Lawrence X. Chutney divorced his wife Clarice in order to marry his mother-in-law, Marilyn. "Clarice is a good kid," he said with great affection about his ex-spouse, "and I hope she makes me an obedient stepdaughter."

❖   ❖   ❖

In reading over this last morsel, Joey Adams recalled the old one about the fellow who divorced his wife and married his sister-in-law. Seems he was too lazy to break in a new mother-in-law.

❖   ❖   ❖

Believe it or not (and I've been trying to check this one out for months), but a Laredo, Texas, lawyer sponsored a bowling tournament between the Optimist Club and the Junior Chamber of Commerce. And you know what he offered as a door prize? A free divorce!

11

Be Nice, Now . . .

ETIQUETTE is a funny unwritten law about which many people have written books, performed television shows, given lectures, and been interviewed on tevee and radio programs. Etiquette in boxing is shaking hands before you belt the other fellow's block off. Etiquette in social circles is to ac-

cept an invitation to be bored at someone else's cocktail party so you, in turn, can invite her to be bored at one of your cocktail parties. Etiquette is calling someone Miss or Mrs. when what you really mean is madam. And you know full well what a madam is. There are all sorts of interpretations on exactly what constitutes an act of etiquette, but in this particular batch of news stories I think you'll agree that even etiquette can be carried too far.

❖ ❖ ❖

For example, let's take this gruesome wire-service story. "Philip Jones," it starts off innocently enough, "a mild-mannered clerk, has signed a confession to the decapitation slaying of his wife. Jones confessed he had severed his wife's head with a saw. Asked what he had done with her head, Jones said: 'Well, it's almost too terrible to tell; but here's the truth: I burned Dorothy's head in the incinerator at home.' Asked when he did the burning, the clerk replied: 'Why, in the morning, of course. It's against the law to burn anything in your incinerator after noon.'" See what I mean? Even some murderers conform to the rules of etiquette!

❖ ❖ ❖

For some strange reason many lawbreakers, who don't care who they kill, maim, kidnap or mug, have an instinct to observe certain social graces. Such an instance occurred in Detroit when a poor and lonely cab driver was held up and robbed of $8 and a cheap wrist watch. Looking over his frugal loot the stickupman returned everything, plus $2 of his own, saying: "Things ain't too good with you, bud; here, buy some cigarettes and coffee, you look nervous."

❖ ❖ ❖

Despite all the bank robberies going on these days (the F.B.I. notes this particular crime has gone up some 400 percent) the boys aren't all bad. A lone gunman held up a savings banks in Iowa, grabbed off some $12,000 (using a Luger as a withdrawal slip), and as he tied up the cashier whispered, "I hate this kind of work, but what with taxes and alimony and stuff like that a guy can't make an honest living these days."

❖ ❖ ❖

Even Willie "The Actor" Sutton, probably the best known bank robber of our time, had a soft spot. After his last escapade Willie was given a sentence totaling some 135 years. With time off for good behavior he'd be eligible for parole in New York State sometime around 2036, in the spring of the year. And at that time he'd be picked up to finish a sentence (or maybe it was more like a paragraph) that he started but neglected to finish in the neighboring state of New Jersey. In any event, after he was incarcerated for his final term, Willie got religion and together with his lawyer decided that whatever funds he had or which might accrue from movies or books to be written around his nefarious career, be devoted to helping paroled criminals go straight. In naming trustees for his estate, the bank robber included one of the officials of the Manufacturers Trust Company in Long Island, a branch he had robbed. "I think," he explained to his lawyer, "I owe those people a little something."

❖   ❖   ❖

Even petty thieves are magnanimous when it comes to observing etiquette. Up in Bangor, Maine, two suits were stolen from a long-time local resident. The next night the same burglar broke into the same house and risked apprehension by returning the two suits. Attached to one of the suits was this explanatory note: "The colors don't match my eyes. And besides they don't fit too good."

❖   ❖   ❖

Sometimes there's a trace of irony in a theft. Take the burglar who entered the home of a woman in Canoga Park, Calif., while she was busy getting a divorce from her husband. Only one item was missing when the happy woman came home with the divorce decree in her purse—her wedding ring.

❖   ❖   ❖

My favorite in this department concerns a rather pathetic note which appeared in a Brooklyn neighborhood newspaper in the "Personals" column. "To Whom It may concern: I'll give a $10 reward, no questions asked, for anyone in the Coney Island area who finds a pair of brass knuckles I lost.

They ain't worth nothing to you, but to me there's a big sentimental value. Look on inside for inscription: 'From Beth to Pete with Love.'"

❖   ❖   ❖

A column contributor forwarded this morsel some months ago. It reported thieves breaking into an apartment tenanted by a young woman in Fort Worth, Tex., and helping themselves to $26 in cash, some of those hideous sack dresses, a plate of frozen spaghetti and meatballs, and two bottles of gin. The intruders were thoughtful enough, however, before taking it on the lam, to get a brush and varnish and touch up the back door which they had splintered when they forced entry.

❖   ❖   ❖

San Francisco has the nicest trolley motormen. Noticing his passengers perspiring with the heat, motorman number 1352 parked his trolley, went into a drug store, and bought ice cream sundaes for all his passengers.

❖ ❖ ❖

As frightening as an intruder in the night must be, a secretary in Altoona, Pa., wouldn't mind at all socially meeting a burglar who awakened her at 3 o'clock one morning and demanded her cash. When informed that all she had in the house was $6, the housebreaker gazed into her eyes, said she had an honest face, and apologized for waking her up. "I'm sorry, miss," he said, looking at his notebook. "I musta had the wrong address. The joint I cased is across the street."

❖ ❖ ❖

Another thief, maybe kin to the soft-hearted burglar in Altoona, broke into the Cowles Bakery in Dayton, Ohio, along with a henchman. Before they left they brewed some coffee, partook of some cake, and then washed the dishes.

❖ ❖ ❖

Something similar occurred in Oakland, Calif., when a thief removed a whole sun parlor full of potted plants. But before running off with the pots, he carefully planted the flowers in the front lawn.

❖ ❖ ❖

Another pair of warm-hearted bandits held up a Los Angeles market, and after rifling the day's receipts pushed two butchers into the cold storage plant. Before leaving the scene of the crime, one of the mugs telephoned the police and suggested they rush over slowly, open the icebox and possibly prevent their victims from catching pneumonia.

❖   ❖   ❖

Sometimes etiquette shows itself in the form of consideration. Take the safecrackers who did a neat job of blowing
up a blowup-proof safe in a Zanesville, Ohio, supermarket.
Separating the cash from ordinary business papers, before
they departed they left the firm's burglary policy on top
of the safe.

❖   ❖   ❖

Etiquette has various connotations, as you'll admit when
you digest this little item. When Dean Hoffman of Pennsylvania State University retired some time ago, he made a confession to friends. He revealed that some 40 years previously
he was the student who dumped a bucket of water on
faculty members.

❖   ❖   ❖

Which slides neatly into this classic morsel: "Students at
Montana State University," their weekly newspaper an-
nounced, "will stage an annual 'Be Kind to the Faculty
Day.'"

❖   ❖   ❖

Even the Internal Revenue Service isn't immune to receiving an occasional olive branch in the form of a letter.
The Washington office received the following note: "I
cheated on my income tax return two years ago and haven't
had a good night's sleep since. Consequently I'm enclosing
a check for $28 and if I find I still can't sleep I'll send you
the balance."

❖   ❖   ❖

This was just a coincidence, but I'll wager you couldn't
prove that to the motorist involved. He was held up on a

lonesome Wyoming state road, beaten, robbed, and left lying, unconscious, against a wooden sign. When he woke up he blinked, because the message on the sign read: "The Chamber of Commerce Thanks You for Visiting Us—Come Again."

❖　❖　❖

Then there's the Philadelphia father who was dragged to court by his spouse accused of going on a bat with the boys and leaving their 2-year-old son asleep in his crib with a butcher knife under his pillow. "I wanted to give Ned something to play with in case he woke up," the thoughtful (?) dad explained, "but I was afraid if I left my gun he'd wake up the neighbors."

❖　❖　❖

Railroad men still talk about how considerate the Union Pacific is. As evidence of this consideration they refer to the time a snowstorm prevented the crack train, The City of St. Louis, from continuing on to its destination. Realizing they'd be stuck for hours, maybe days, the conductors and the engineer got together and agreed to back the train out of dry Kansas into wet Colorado so the bar could be legally opened.

❖　❖　❖

Robert Dowling, president of the City Investment Trust and dozens of other important firms, likes to tell about a letter the automobile finance company received along with the twenty-fourth and final payment of a car owner. It was a brief, but pungent, postscript saying: "Sincerely, but no longer yours. . . ."

❖   ❖   ❖

Reno police observe etiquette on St. Valentine's Day by
giving parking violators a holiday. Instead of tucking tickets
underneath the windshield wipers, they slip this little bit
of verse under the rubber: "Won't you be our Valentine, and
help us with our work? You'll save yourself a fine, dear
friend, and a visit to our clerk!"

❖   ❖   ❖

Sometimes the trend is reversed. Like the Carmel, N.Y.,
pharmacy which was robbed of 200 fountain pens. The next
day the proprietor bought space in the local newspaper to
remind the robbers that the pens carried a lifetime guarantee
and to be sure to bring them in for free servicing.

❖   ❖   ❖

Columnist Ollie James in the *Cincinnati Enquirer* went all
the way to Massachusetts to observe this rude but humorous
warning on the front of a roadblock: "Road Closed—Do Not

Enter!" On the back of the same sign was another message:
"Welcome Back, Stupid!"

❖   ❖   ❖

I'll leave you with one final note in the category of etiquette, folks. How cockeyed a world can this be when
thieves in Toronto can break into a laundry truck, steal 35
bags of soiled diapers, and within five days return hundreds
of the diapers washed and ready for use?

12

How's That Again, Bud?

WITHOUT any organized lobby to make a big fuss about it, I think there are more boner hunters across the nation than there are duck hunters, bird watchers, golfers, bowlers, or even television critics.

It's a mighty thrifty pastime in which to participate. No license is required. No muscle flexing is necessary. On a lucky safari you can bag a collection of beauties from a sitting position.

All you need do to go boner hunting is to buy, borrow, or purloin your favorite daily or weekly newspaper, arm yourself with grandpa's specs or a 15-cent magnifying glass, and start wading through the personal columns, classified ads, and social announcements.

Because newspapers are manufactured with such great speed to keep hot news from getting cold, even the most meticulous of newspaper compositors, headline writers, rewrite men, and proof readers occasionally slip a disc. Sometimes the slips in the night loom loud or raucous the next morning. Frequently they're funny, sometimes they're too lewd to laugh at in public. These latter boners then become collector's items and eventually crumble into confetti from being passed so often from one sweaty palm to another.

Next to active boner hunting (more wicked than cricket) are the radio reporters, vest-pocket-sized magazines, and columnists who repeat or reprint these minor mistakes for the edification of their listeners or readers. As a consequence the actual sources of the boners, or quaintly juxtapositioned phrases, are frequently lost as they shuffle from pillage to post office. So we won't make even a feeble attempt to document or guarantee the authenticity of the prize examples we group together on the following pages.

❖　❖　❖

We'll tee off with an ad we actually picked up eight or nine vacations ago up in the Berkshire Hills of Massachusetts; I believe this appeared in the *Berkshire Evening Eagle*. It concerned an ad pushing a local restaurant's week-end family special. "Roast Native Turkey, $2.50; Southern Fried Chicken, $2.50; Broiled Sirloin Steak, $3.50; Children Under 7 Years, $1.25." (We checked at the time and were told that children over the age of 7 years, like turkeys the same age, are too tough to digest.)

❖   ❖   ❖

In the same mountainous country are many summer camps. A North Adams, Mass., sports page printed the results of a Saturday afternoon game between some girl campers and their male parents. "The camp girls were doing just fine against their fathers," the item reported, "until the last half of the seventh inning when all the bags got loaded." (No mention was made about how loaded their fathers got after the ninth inning!)

❖   ❖   ❖

I don't know where Allendale is, and I don't know how advanced the *Allendale Advance* is. But I do know, because I have the clipping right in front of me, that they really advertised choice four-room apartments at the Shelton Arms of that city. "They're light, airy, provide day and night elevator service, kitchenette, bath and shower and—venetian blonds." . . . (Personally, I prefer Venetian brunettes such as Gina and Sophia.)

❖ ❖ ❖

In New York, the *Corning Leader* society column is supposed to have printed an item about a local couple tossing a birthday party for their 3-year-old daughter at which some 24 children were present. "Mrs. Soandso," the item concludes, with nary a pause for breath, "entered the Wellsboro Hospital the next day for observation."

❖ ❖ ❖

Another story popped up in an Ohio news weekly describing a slight accident and its aftermath. "The front of Mr. B's car," it explained, "struck Miss R. in the rear. He immediately picked her up, felt her all over to make sure she was in one piece, and when she smiled and said thanks, was encouraged to take her home where he could examine her even more intimately." (No report of what Mrs. B had to say about Mr. B's first or second aid.)

❖ ❖ ❖

A similar item appeared in a Shreveport newspaper, equally spiced, reporting, "The driver of the offending car said it wasn't his fault, that the reason he smashed into Miss E————'s rear was because it was sticking out into the roadway." (He's lucky it was a live, not a dead-end street.)

❖ ❖ ❖

A newspaper in Birmingham had its political reporter attend a housewives' function at which one of the city's high officials made the main speech. He was quoted as saying "Our morality rate is low while our birth rate is high."

❖   ❖   ❖

Speaking of birth rates, a Carbondale, Pa., radio announcer got all excited and told listeners, "It was a mixed-up day at the carnival. More than 67 youngsters were lost. Luckily, however, they were returned to their parents through the loudspeaker system." (Luckily, the loud-speaker system was large enough to accommodate such heavy traffic.)

❖   ❖   ❖

This was palmed off as a linotypist's error: "Mr. and Mrs. Harold and Alice Z——s flew to Rochester, Minn., yesterday where Molly expects to have a garter removed by one of the Mayos." (Isn't that stretching a garter too far?)

❖   ❖   ❖

What started out to be a sentimental notice of a sixty-fifth anniversary turned out to be the laugh of the town of Richmond, Va., with this report: "Mr. and Mrs. Jonesy broke the record for bedded bliss. She wore a tailored suit and an orchard corsage. He wore a grin." (You'd grin, too, if you were married to a woman buxom enough to make an orchard look cozy in her cleavage.)

❖   ❖   ❖

Down around South Bend, Ind., I'm told, they're still talking about a paragraph which appeared on the front page of a suburban weekly. "Prizes will be distributed all week at the high school cooking class with a grand prize of a deep freezer. To determine the Big Winner all those who attend Saturday will be shook up in a big box." (I wonder if that's the way Elvis Presley started?)

❖ ❖ ❖

A vocal coach ran this small classified ad in a weekly musical trade paper: "Girls who have ambitions to sing with a band should take vice lessons." (I don't know of any faster way to get a job singing with a band!)

❖ ❖ ❖

The *Reader's Digest,* in a way-back-when edition, to judge by the yellowed paper, reprinted this from the *Malaya Sunday Tribune:* "Mrs. Winston Churchill told members of YWCA committees in Liverpool: 'Ninety percent of the mistresses on YWCA hostel beds are not fit to sleep on.'" (It makes you stop and wonder who auditioned the talent in the Liverpool YWCA.)

❖ ❖ ❖

Heavens to Betsy if this isn't one for the book! I repeat it verbatim from a staid New England journal in which the item appeared: "Held for observation, the attractively shaped prisoner escaped from jail by slipping out of her pajamas. This proved her undoing, however, since it was simple for the police to trail her behind."

❖   ❖   ❖

A cheerier *Digest* reprint came from New Hampshire in the *Portsmouth Herald:* "Here's the recipe for 'French Egg Nog': two egg yolks, two tablespoons of sugar and two jiggers of cognac in a tall warm lass." (How about one jigger in a short warm lass?)

❖   ❖   ❖

Recently we saw a dandy whodunit on television and wrote to ask the producers for a copy of the mystery script. It arrived a few weeks later with a lovely but topically befitting typo on the last page: Copyfright 1958.

❖   ❖   ❖

*(Aside to compositors setting up this chapter: It just oc-
curred to me what a dirty trick you could play on me if you,
by instinct, corrected all the typographical mistakes we're
compounding by reprinting.)* . . .

❖   ❖   ❖

The *Miami Beach Sun,* columnist Paul Bruun says, carried
this eyebrow-raiser on its sports page. Describing a championship golf tournament the over-excited reporter said:
"The surprise of the afternoon was the gallery neglecting
the favorite to follow young Maxine Bennett, whose shorts
kept dropping on the green." (Mr. Bruun's comment: "I'd
like to see more of Miss Bennett in another tournament!")

❖   ❖   ❖

A Grand Rapids newspaper allegedly printed the story of
a small theft at the home of a local schoolteacher. "She said,"
it said, "that the money was concealed in her garter and she
didn't notice her loss until after the departure of a vacuum-
cleaner salesman who aroused her curiosity demonstrating
his line."

❖   ❖   ❖

No country doctor ever received as warm an accolade as
an Ohio obstetrician who was marking his sixtieth anniversary. "Doc Drender," it eulogized, "practiced for more than
sixty years and is responsible for most of the babies born
in this community." (Practiced hell, the Doc was perfect!)

❖   ❖   ❖

Walter Winchell is the authority for this typo which he quoted from his home base newspaper, the *New York Daily Mirror:* "Former Secretary of State Dean Acheson arrived for a sex-week vacation."

❖   ❖   ❖

The *Louisville Times* carried this classic: ". . . He was the victim of a cute nervous dyspepsia." (They didn't say what the cutie's first name was.)

❖   ❖   ❖

In the tornado country, a weekly newspaper listed the deaths, injuries, and property damages left in the wake of a twister, and concluded with this item: "The twister carried off Ben Jenson's house and furniture and all three of his children. Neighbors donated a new bed to give Ben and his wife a fresh start."

❖   ❖   ❖

A similar item appeared in a Puerto Rico newspaper after a hurricane hit. "At the home of Jose deBlanca Herrera, only part of his wife's bedroom remained standing. And when Jose removed the bed mattress he was surprised to find a pair of pants that did not belong to him or anyone else in his housing project." (It's an ill wind . . . and so on!)

cigarettes, candy, cooking facilities, and, in extreme instances, marijuana cigarettes and even prostitutes. Some of the boys also look upon certain prisons as alma maters. For example, a semi-permanent resident of a Florida state prison, who pitched for his cellblock ball team for a half dozen years, was told, in the middle of a no-hit game, to report for his parole. He was so incensed he threw the ball at a guard, the rest of his teammates started to riot and the whole team was tossed into solitary. Naturally, the pitcher didn't have to worry any longer about a parole. His teammates were assured he'd be around for at least another three seasons.

❖   ❖   ❖

Just a short while ago a chap named Early Gray, convicted in Boston of a minor crime, nearly had his lawyer tearing his hair out when the defendant pleaded with the judge to give him a longer term than the 18 months announced. Gray didn't like the city prison to which short termers were sent because, he said, "The State Prison has a better athletic program." The judge offered his full cooperation and gave Earl a three year sentence, tantamount to an athletic scholarship.

❖   ❖   ❖

Former Sullivan, N.Y., County Judge Moses Kove, who served so admirably at the Nuremberg trials, delights in telling this story about a case in which a friend of his was involved. The friend, a judge with a fine sense of humor, told Moe that he recently had a very unusual experience. "A few days before a trial started, the plaintiff's lawyer," he explained, "gave me a Thunderbird Convertible. And, before I even found a parking space for the T-Bird, the defendant's lawyer had a Cadillac delivered to my door." "In that case," Kove said, "what did you do?" "I did what any honest judge would do," the jurist replied, throwing out his chest and looking respectably indignant. "I decided the case on its merits!"

❖   ❖   ❖

Despite the austerity of the average court and the reluctance on the part of any judge to countenance horseplay or tomfoolery when he's wearing the robe, the day-to-day routine can become awfully boring. And either a lawyer or a litigant with a sense of humor often lightens the load.

Many such instances are on the record. This one for instance, happened in a Baltimore court. A witness raised her left hand to be sworn in. The clerk insisted she raise her right hand. "This is my right hand," she told the Judge, ignoring the clerk. "I'm left handed."

❖   ❖   ❖

A real puzzler cropped up in the City of Brotherly Love when the Philadelphia city solicitor's office got in the act. They insisted, upon threat of court action, that a certain Harry Zeitz fork up $5.35 in delinquent taxes. They dropped the case when it was discovered that the gentleman in question was in prison awaiting the carrying out of a death sentence. (In this instance, poor H.Z. was facing both death and taxes in his last breath.)

❖   ❖   ❖

Myles Lane tried explaining how such a decision as the one rendered in Iowa some time ago is possible. A bride-to-be actually was awarded a $6,000 judgment in a "breach of promise" suit based on the fact that her fiancé passed away before the wedding.

❖   ❖   ❖

There must be something to feminine charm. A chorus gal in a New York nightclub, suing a man for $4,000 in damages for insulting her, looked so hurt in her skin-tight dress the all-male jury awarded her $5,500. (Obviously the damages didn't show.)

❖   ❖   ❖

Another charmer, a South Carolina housewife, was arrested in the morning and acquitted in the afternoon for hitting a belligerent bill collector over the noggin with a baseball bat. The magistrate, who probably bought a few things on the installment plan himself, offered his congratulations and said if he could have he would have given her a medal.

❖   ❖   ❖

Silliest edict ever handed down in Minot, N. Dak., or anywhere else for that matter, was a judge ordering Theodore Baker, up on a charge of driving without a license, to go out and get a license. What for? So the state could revoke it forthwith!

❖   ❖   ❖

Most sensible decision ever rendered, at least in my opinion, was that of a Sunnyvale, Calif., traffic court judge. He got so tired over a defendant's two-hour insistence of innocence that he dismissed the bore and paid the fine himself.

❖   ❖   ❖

The Albuquerque, N. Mex., District Court had a lulu on its hands when a fellow named George Peter Janetakos petitioned to have his name changed. He preferred to be known as George Bill Janetakos.

❖   ❖   ❖

This recalls a similar situation back in the dark days when Adolph Hitler was ruining the world. A chap named Stinker asked the court for permission to change his name. "With the name Stinker," the court agreed, "I don't blame you." "You don't seem to understand," Mr. Stinker pleaded, "I don't want to change my last name. I want to change my first name—it's Adolph!"

❖   ❖   ❖

A Detroit judge was amused, then annoyed, when a motorist, appearing before him on a charge of drunken driving pleaded the Fifth Amendment. "You'll have to dig up a new Amendment," hizzoner snapped. "You've already drunk up the Fifth."

❖   ❖   ❖

In an almost parallel situation in Chicago, the traffic court judge admonished a defendent for pleading the Fifth Amendment: "You must be watching too much television!"

❖   ❖   ❖

I can't attest to the veracity of this incident, but commentator Barry Gray insists it happened in a small southern town. The wife of a very popular local figure was fined for failing to curb her dog. Not having sufficient cash, she started to write out a check. "You look awfully nervous," the kind judge said as he noticed her hands trembling. "Perhaps you'd rather pay later." "Not at all, thank you," the wife said, "I'm completely composed." Whereupon she handed the clerk a check properly made out in every detail except one. Instead of her own name, she'd signed the judge's name!

❖   ❖   ❖

Remember that old wheeze Milton Berle used to pull out of a hat whenever he was in a hotel and someone with an odd name like Pheffingerstahl was paged? Berle would yell out "What are the initials?" Well, this fits into that category. A petty thief, caught in the act of finding a purse before it was lost, told the Lancaster, Calif., police his name was Joshua Heitize Baussloipezkuffbergarzime. (He was probably acquitted because there wasn't a clerk in town who could pronounce his name.)

❖   ❖   ❖

That ancient adage about politics making strange bedfellows was certainly never better demonstrated than when a Milwaukee fellow was arrested for stealing a local councilman's car. "I had a right to it," he insisted. "I voted for the guy, didn't I?"

❖   ❖   ❖

This makes more horse sense: a fellow in a suburb of Paris (France, that is) was arrested for stealing a horse. "I'm guilty with an explanation," he told the court. "You see I had to do it to help my asthma and cigarette cough. When I sit atop a horse the altitude permits me to breathe easier." The judge didn't mind the defendant's altitude, but gave him 60 days to alter his attitude.

❖   ❖   ❖

I'm sure most of us who have inhibitions would often just love to pick up a brick and throw it through the window of a nasty neighbor's house, or muss up the slicked-down hair of a sharpie. Well, then, if you were the judge what would you do if a fellow was brought before you on charges of tossing a hunk of concrete through a police station glass door? I guess you'd do exactly what a San Mateo, Calif., magistrate did when the defendant upped and admitted "I had to do this—it's been building up in me for 30 years!" You'd make him pay damages and dismiss charges.

❖   ❖   ❖

Some people don't have any luck. Take the screwball arrested at 3 o'clock one morning for offering his Bronx subway seat to a woman. Only two hitches marred the man's courteous act. Number one: He and she were the only two people in the car at the time. Two: She happened to be a policewoman!

❖   ❖   ❖

You'd be amazed how many people get away with anything short of murder when they're honest enough to admit the truth when facing a judge. Take the character in Nashville, Tenn., who was hauled into court dripping with blood from wounds incurred in a free-for-all razor fight. When the judge suggested that in the future he stay out of trouble by keeping out of bad company, he said "That ain't possible, judge, I haven't got enough money to buy me a divorce."

❖ ❖ ❖

Because of all the muggings and mayhem going on in the shadows of what could be one of the most beautiful areas in New York, Central Park, the area is frequently patrolled by teams of detectives, one in his regular clothes, the other in female attire. To nab unwary stickupmen, the two detectives sit on park benches and simulate necking. One such detective got tired of playing the role of a gal and asked his precinct captain please to give him another assignment or an extra day off a week. "It takes me that much longer," he complained, "to get in and out of these damned dresses and things."

❖ ❖ ❖

What tries the patience of some judges are petty cases, usually inspired by pique on the part of the plaintiff. In a recent case, Mrs. Mary Petrula, an Iowa City laundress, brought suit against Jamesy Waschkil for $1,196 covering 20 years of washing his shirts at $1 per week. (Wonder if Waschkil tried to settle for 20 years' worth of broken buttons?)

❖ ❖ ❖

Here's one that'll burn you up even reading about it happening to someone else. In Los Angeles, a Mrs. Marge Davies spent five months in the hospital from injuries sustained when she was hit by a car. Carried into court on a stretcher, Mrs. Davies was fined $25 for jaywalking.

❖   ❖   ❖

Slapsie Maxie Rosenbloom walked against a "Don't Walk" sign and was stopped by a traffic cop who said, "You blind? It says 'Don't Walk' and you walk. I'm gonna give you a ticket." As he wrote out the summons, Maxie asked, "Officer, tell me, how fast was I going?"

❖   ❖   ❖

Names make odd news, even if the "crime" is minor. Take the Madison, Wis., lady who was arrested some time ago on charges of being a public drunk. The item wouldn't have seen the light of day if it wasn't for the fact that the defendant's name happened to be Drinkwater.

❖   ❖   ❖

Speaking of imbibers, a McKeesport, Pa., woman took ten days in the clink for driving an unlicensed vehicle while drunk. The vehicle happened to be a power lawnmower.

❖   ❖   ❖

Julius LaRosa clipped this out of *Coronet* because he thought it was one of the most amusing court cases he had ever read about. As the magazine's word juggler wrote it, a girl in Ohio, by the artful use of a pair of spectacles, kept her fiance from finding out that she had a glass eye. He insisted that nullified the marriage contract and took the case to court. This was the decision: "It is not necessary for a girl during courtship to inform her intended husband of any device or attachment used to improve the work of nature in the construction of her face or figure."

❖   ❖   ❖

Recall that old Dorothy Parker bit of verse that went "Men never make passes at girls who wear glasses"? Well, it isn't true. In a home for unmarried mothers, a spy informs us that 65 per cent of the house guests wear spectacles.

❖   ❖   ❖

Which recalls the story of a young man who told his draft board that he was 4-F because of faulty eyesight. To prove his point he brought his wife along.

❖   ❖   ❖

Silliest case of 1959 (this happened in Los Angeles in May), actually wasn't a case at all. The F.B.I. merely picked up a fellow named William Donald McKeown on suspicion —and confirmed the suspicion when, in searching Donald's pockets they discovered a "Wanted" circular with the hapless defendant's picture printed thereon.

❖ ❖ ❖

A case of unmistaken identity was recorded in Boston. A criminal, wanted in five states, was picked up by local police when he thoughtlessly registered in a hotel under the name of a pal. The pal also happened to be on the police wanted list.

❖ ❖ ❖

Probably the most surprised man in Memphis was a hit-and-run truck driver who hit a car driven by LeMoyne College student Louis Martin. Louis, 18, and a letterman who won his honors as a top quarter-miler, chased his assailant for two blocks on foot and held on to him until police came.

❖ ❖ ❖

And *Jet*, the weekly magazine, reported an oddity from Detroit. When a chap named Moses Bray, Jr., 19, attempted to settle an argument over a cigarette between William Woods, 17, and King Chandler, 15, at a teenage party, he was fatally stabbed by a 15-year-old bystander. This wouldn't be much of an item, since it happens too often these days, except that in this instance the knife-wielding juvenile's name was George Washington.

14

You're Only Young Twice

IF ALL THE YOUNGSTERS said and did all the funny things
their parents say the youngsters say and do there'd be no
teenage problem. For you can't laugh and engage in mayhem on the same whirl. Humor, which usually rides around
in cycles just like the plots of movies, tevee shows, and
books, sometimes is pretty cruel. For example, one popular
source of merriment these days centers on the unhappy and
necessarily abnormal offspring of picture stars whose favorite
pastime seems to be taking frequent rides on the marry-go-
'round.

Typical of this type of humor is the story Linda Darnell
tells about the much-married Hollywood couple who celebrated their first anniversary at home with their six children
—three of his, two of hers, and one of theirs!

❖ ❖ ❖

Peter Lorre has a different version of this yarn. It concerns a little girl whose stepfather staged a sixth birthday
party for her to which her real father dropped in. The doll

139

was so glad to see the unexpected visitor she threw her arms around him, gave him a big kiss, and then said: "Gosh I'm happy to see you again, sir. Won't you please sign my guest register?"

❖   ❖   ❖

Mike Stern, the unofficial mayor of Rome, Italy, flew to the West Coast to visit with some movie friends and ran into two youngsters playing in the living room. The 7-year-old girl, daughter of Mike's three-times-married hostess, was playing house with the 6-year-old son of his twice-married host. "Let's play house, Sally," the boy said. "I'll play a psychiatrist, you be the wife with the problem, and my friend Mike here will be the divorce lawyer!"

❖   ❖   ❖

Emmett Kelley, one of the most beloved of all circus clowns, likes to recall the days when the Ringling Circus played under canvas. "Whenever we went on the road," Emmett explained, "we knew that dozens of kids would try to sneak into the Big Tent. While the management let the small fry in the front entrance, for free if they were underprivileged youngsters, we knew that psychologically it would be more exciting for them if they thought they were getting away with something. Consequently there was always a "constable" who chased them when he caught them slipping under the canvas. But he never caught anyone. The reason? The "constable" was just a clown giving the boys and girls a run for their lack of money.

❖   ❖   ❖

Way out West where men are men and women sometimes rough up other women, a middle-aged housewife, of

Stockton, Calif., had her leg broken by a daughter-in-law. Explained the unhappy mother-in-law: "Sheilah got mad because I refused to baby-sit her five children five nights a week."

❖ ❖ ❖

Gene Baylos, the very funny comedian, is particularly fond of a young niece. The other day the little girl proudly showed her uncle a memorandum from her singing teacher explaining that while she can't sing well she helps along the rest of the students by being an attentive listener. To a comedian, who adores listeners much more than talkers, especially if they're listening to him, this report makes his niece *Time* Magazine's Girl of the Year.

❖ ❖ ❖

Oddity from Onerahi, New Zealand: The school buses in the vicinity carry posters on the sides advertising Teacher's Whiskey. "It helps to pay part of the cost of the drivers," we're told.

❖ ❖ ❖

Teenagers come in for their share of fun also. Take Alan King's observation that it's ridiculous to criticize the way they talk on the 'phone. "By the time they hang up, they're often in their twenties."

❖ ❖ ❖

And Sam Levenson tells about a young college student who returned home for the Christmas holidays sporting a pair of the brightest-hued shiners he'd ever seen, together with a gashed cheek and a sore jaw. When asked what hap-

141

pened he shrugged and said, "A little odd accident. Seems I was sitting in the grass with my girl when I was run over by a rabbit."

❖   ❖   ❖

Bud Collyer's college son sent a letter to the folks which Mrs. Collyer started to read aloud but was stopped midway by Bud who said: "Forget the details, darling, just get to the part that says 'By the way, Dad.'"

❖   ❖   ❖

The 7-year-olds are brighter than brass buttons. Take Larry Gore's youngster Billy, for example—and Larry would like you to take him for awhile. The other evening when dad and mom were coding their conversation via the spelling system, Billy interrupted and asked: "How are you folks going to talk to each other about me when I learn to spell?"

❖   ❖   ❖

Wilbur Clark of the Desert Inn in Las Vegas wondered why one of his casino croupiers was handing out cigars the other day. "Have a baby, Jim?" he asked. "Nope, sir," was the reply. "I just got the good news that I WON'T be a father!"

❖　❖　❖

Morsels, or filler items, concerning children or dogs are always welcomed by editors. They add a touch of warmth to the cold print of hard news. Here are some of my favorites in that department.

A sign in a Portland, Maine, toy store reads: "Ideal gift to noisy children—BREAKABLE RECORDS!"

❖　❖　❖

Bob Strong saw this one over a display of blue jeans in a Birmingham teenage shop: "Guaranteed to shrink!"

❖　❖　❖

Teddy's, one of New York's most famous Italian restaurants, doesn't exactly go in for the kiddie trade, but its host, Sal Cucinotta, has made some concession to parents who can't find baby sitters. In small type, right on the back of his menu, Sal offers half-price for any children who stay glued to the table while a parent feeds them.

❖　❖　❖

Charley Morris, an old pal of ours, related this true tale to us. A Newark mother, worried because her 9-year-old daughter kept losing weight, took her to a psychiatrist. After a few hours of seemingly inconsequential conversation the medic came up with the answer. It seems the youngster had been reading—and following—one of mother's books, a diet best-seller titled *How to Lose a Pound a Day.*

❖　❖　❖

John Cronin, at one time head of the Missing Persons
Bureau in the Bronx, found himself in the uncomfortable
position one day of having to hunt for his own two children.
After many hours he located them hiding behind a tombstone in a nearby cemetery. When asked what the big idea
was, the youngsters chuckled and said "Dad, we wanted to
see how quickly you could find missing persons."

❖　❖　❖

To motorists who practically live in their cars, the story
of young Henry Simpson the Third, of Atlanta, will be
amusing. Henry the Second tossed a first birthday party for
the boy right in the back seat of the Buick where he was
born.

❖　❖　❖

There's a city in Michigan with a name that sounds more
like punctuation than anything else, namely Onekama. Anyway the head of the Consolidated School in Onekama has a
delicious sense of humor. And to prove it he sent a note to

parents, clipped to the monthly report cards, reading: "Please examine, grit your teeth silently, sign, and return report cards immediately."

❖   ❖   ❖

A delightful true story broke in a Cleveland newspaper recently. It told about a doting mother whose 13-year-old son looted his dad's new-car fund and spent the $8 going to the movies, bowling, taking his best girl out for sodas, and spending the remaining $2 to buy two raffle tickets on a new car. The "crime" wasn't discovered until two weeks later when a stranger telephoned mother and asked where to deliver the new Lincoln her son won.

❖   ❖   ❖

Every once in a while one of those "crime doesn't pay" stories boomerangs, such as in the tale above and in one that happened in Atlantic City. Here a teacher, taking her class to a drug store for a quick luncheon, noticed that one young lad was fascinated by a nickel slot machine. She proceeded to give the entire group a lecture on the futility of trying to beat such a machine, then deposited a nickel to prove her point. I'll bet you think you know the answer —that she hit the jackpot? Well, she didn't. She lost the nickel and everybody lived happily ever after.

❖   ❖   ❖

Hal March, who helped to start the big money quiz show craze, has a favorite story. It dates back to the early days of Hal's top show when he made a personal appearance down in Texas and noticed that in Dallas the "$64,000 Question" was listed under "Children's Programs."

❖   ❖   ❖

Which recalls the Texan who gave his 5-year-old son a jack-in-the-box with real jack in it.

❖   ❖   ❖

That's the same fellow who, Jan Murray insists, when his son wanted trains for Christmas, bought him the New York Central.

❖   ❖   ❖

I didn't mean to get off on a Texas kick, but since we started let's throw in Roger Price's silly-dilly about the wealthy Texan who refused to bother switching to filter cigarettes. He had a filter built into his throat.

❖   ❖   ❖

Ralph Gardner looked up a local Long Island directory of baby-sitters and was intrigued by one which carried this word of caution: "If your children won't mind you, don't ask us to mind them."

❖   ❖   ❖

There are a number of fine rural schools in Kansas, one of which, on the outskirts of Junction City, flaunts a large red and white sign reading: "Please Drive Carefully. Don't run over the children. Wait for the teacher."

❖   ❖   ❖

Funny incident occurred in Dartford, England. Exhibitors staging a display of new ideas in office machines and equipment couldn't understand why so many people of school age kept streaming into the hall until they found out the kids were doing all their homework on the adding machines.

❖   ❖   ❖

And a family, living off one of the fairways on the Englewood, N.J., golf course, has posted a sign that makes conversation: "We are trying to raise two young boys beyond this fence. So please, golfers, try to avoid enriching their vocabularies."

❖　❖　❖

George DeWitt revisited the public school which he attended some years ago in Chicago, and sat in the rear while the teacher instructed the class in the morning's activity. Told to go to the blackboard and write a very brief sentence on the subject of a self-evident truth, one youngster raised his hand, picked up a piece of chalk and wrote: "School stinks."

❖　❖　❖

The Associated Press datelined this dandy, Cumberland, R.I., and it was cute enough to make the front pages of many newspapers including the *New York Journal-American.* "The 84 boys and girls 'graduating' from a kindergarten class," the dispatch read, "were drilled to say 'Thank you, Mr. Nevins' when Supt. Vincent Nevins presented them diplomas. But Nevins was unable to attend the ceremony and Miss Lillian I. Hannan, the principal, substituted for him. The first 83 children in line bowed to Miss Hannan, but said 'Thank you, Mr. Nevins.' The 84th kindergartener came close to being correct. She knew there was something wrong somewhere and ad-libbed 'Thank you, *Mrs.* Nevins.'"

15

Oops, Sorreeee

EVERYBODY MAKES MISTAKES, big people, small people, important people, unknown folks. That's why they put sneakers on hotel detectives. In this chapter we'll go into some of the more amusing situations growing out of mistakes.

❖   ❖   ❖

Jack Dempsey and the man who took his heavyweight title, Gene Tunney, are good friends these days, happy to run into each other, quick to embrace, mutual in their respect and affection. But it wasn't always such a lovey-dovey relationship. The heavyweight title is a rare and precious treasure, and it isn't easy to be a gracious loser. Especially since there was some question, in their first bout, whether Jack might not have retained his championship if the referee hadn't started counting over Tunney three or four beats later than he should have.

In any event, shortly after losing the title, the Manassa Mauler picked up a few blue chips by barnstorming across the country refereeing wrestling bouts. On one such hop the matches didn't work out as rehearsed, one brawny bozo threw his opponent in 10 minutes instead of taking 40 minutes to accomplish the gargantuan feat. That gave Dempsey an opportunity to make an earlier train out of Fargo, N. Dak., than he had anticipated. However, getting a berth on the earlier train proved to be a problem until the conductor found the Champ's face familiar and gave him a roomette evidently kept vacant for a train crew poker game.

Early in the morning a knock on the door aroused the champ. Sleepily he climbed out of his berth, opened the door a crack, and came face-to-face with the conductor. The latter explained that he was getting off at the next stop and would be so proud if his celebrated guest gave him an autograph. "I want you to know," he told Dempsey, "what a privilege it is to have you aboard my train, Mr. Tunney." Jack gasped, grinned good-naturedly, then signed the autograph: "To my conductor friend, who never forgets a face. Yours sincerely, Gene Tunney."

❖   ❖   ❖

A charming boo-boo was reported by UPI from Milan, Italy. A beggar, posing as a deaf mute, was arrested when he became involved in a dispute with a streetcar conductor and started yelling.

❖   ❖   ❖

This sort of incident is repeated every once in awhile and always makes the filler banks of newspaper composing rooms waiting for a chance to be published. Down in Alexandria, La., house wreckers parked in front of the home of the Davis residence. Finding no one at home, they proceeded to demolish the place as instructed. By the time Mr. Davis returned home there was only half a home to return to. The wreckers did a perfectly workmanlike job of tearing off the roof, but made only one slight mistake—they had the wrong address.

❖   ❖   ❖

In a similar incident, a firm of house movers picked the wrong house to move, plunked the whole shebang on their trailer and were merrily on their way to another city when the missing house was reported to police. They discovered it off Route 1, 26 miles out of Boston, parked overnight while the truckmen slept in the master bedroom, blissfully unaware that they had a hot house on their hands.

❖   ❖   ❖

And right plumb on Times Square, a blind beggar was arrested when he removed his dark glasses and tenderly and thoughtfully removed a speck from his seeing eye dog's right eye.

❖   ❖   ❖

In Newark, a pair of steeplejacks nimbly shinnied up a four-story-tall smokestack and began to demolish it brick by brick. A couple of thousand bricks later they realized they'd trapped themselves by throwing the bricks inside instead of outside the smokestack, thus blocking the only door through which they could make their exit.

❖   ❖   ❖

News of an unusual sort was made in Los Angeles by Clyde McCall, known as the Sleepy Burglar. He broke into a woman's home, fell asleep, and when awakened by the victim's scream told police he dreamed he was entering his grandmother's house to get a bite of fried chicken when the scream rudely interrupted him.

❖   ❖   ❖

This incident also concerns a hungry thief. He broke into a Toledo drugstore and nibbled on a bottle of sleeping pills marked peppermint drops. He was found unconscious the next morning and rushed to the hospital where the doctors pumped his stomach before detectives pumped his brain.

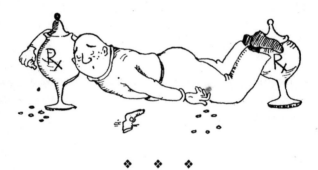

❖   ❖   ❖

A young man named Van Winkle left his father's home in Bloomingburg, N.Y., some years ago, then decided to return without notice. Police, wondering who was occupying the house, investigated, found the son, checked his story and finally withdrew a charge of disorderly conduct. Seems that in his absence pop sold the house.

❖   ❖   ❖

Which brings us to a housekeeper in Little Rock, who won a prize for roasting the shiniest looking chicken ever to be entered into a cooking contest. She lost the prize when it was discovered that she had basted the roasting chicken with shellac.

❖ ❖ ❖

Very often, at night ballgames or trotting races, you hear the announcer say, plaintively: "Attention owner of New York license plate 4G1541. You parked your car properly. You locked it up properly. But you forgot one thing. You forgot to turn off your headlights!" Well, a sportscaster in Tyler, Texas, kept repeating such an announcement recently, then realized to his consternation that the license number he was reciting happened to be his own!

❖ ❖ ❖

And folks in Raleigh might recall the time a café named The Quiet Lunch was closed by police because too many people complained it was too noisy.

❖ ❖ ❖

In Milwaukee, a group of passersby pinned down a young punk who was cuffing about an old, gray-haired woman. When arrested and brought to the station house, the bully's victim pleaded that her attacker be given a suspended sentence. "He told me," the soft-hearted old lady said, "that he's near-sighted and thought he was beating up his mother-in-law."

❖ ❖ ❖

Radio disc jockeys may recall the Springfield, Mass., woman who complained to the authorities that the only sound coming in on her hearing aid was from Radio Station WSFL, located next door.

❖   ❖   ❖

Such incidents aren't as rare as you'd expect, though the explanations bewilder me. In New York City it is frequently reported that certain types of bridgework act as receivers for certain FM radio broadcasts. (Toothpaste sponsors, no doubt.)

❖   ❖   ❖

Artists frequently get into brushes with patronesses. In St. Louis, a woman refused to pay an artist for whom she sat for five weeks, only to have the completed portrait look like her mother, not herself. "She was lucky," the plaintiff's lawyer quoted his client as declaring. "Her mother is better looking than she is."

❖   ❖   ❖

Speaking of painting, some time ago the wife of a friend of ours, who's very finicky about the house, hired a crew of painters to redo all her rooms. To make certain they mixed the right colors she dabbed table tennis paddles with the exact shades she wanted. When she returned home a week later she gave the painters a bonus for the unerring way in which they matched her samples. They accepted the bonuses without telling her that they made many mistakes, but covered up their errors by repainting the paddles to match the walls.

❖   ❖   ❖

Years ago, when Eddie Cantor and George Jessel played vaudeville together, they were frequently asked to appear at charity affairs. On three separate occasions, once at the Astor and twice at the Waldorf, the two comedians discovered that by mistake they entertained the wrong organizations and alienated the affection and friendship of the groups to whom they'd given their word they would appear.

❖   ❖   ❖

On another occasion Jessel was walking into Madison Square Garden when a burly chap pounded him on the back and said, "Eppie, old boy, I'm glad to see you!" Georgie faced his over-enthusiastic back thumper and said angrily: "First of all, I'm not Eppie. Secondly, even if I was Eppie, how dare you hit me that hard?" Now it was the stranger's turn to get angry. "If you're not Eppie," he exclaimed, "what do you care what I do to Eppie!"

❖   ❖   ❖

There are many strange winners of strange contests. Oddest one we know made history in Goulburn, Australia. Here, in a contest to pick the shapeliest legs in town, the contestant who won second place honors was Fred Newton, father of three children.

❖   ❖   ❖

In Tallahassee, Ferdie Q. Kroutman sued a druggist claiming that he was chagrined, annoyed, and frustrated when the chemist bollixed up two prescriptions. This caused him to rub stomach medicine on his scalp and to take a tablespoon of hair tonic three times a day after meals.

❖   ❖   ❖

This happened long about the end of World War II. The Nick Butricks of Shreveport spent weeks trying to find out what happened to the family's car keys, which seemed to have dissolved into thin air. Three weeks after getting a mechanic to dub duplicate keys they received a letter from Holland clearing up the mystery. "Dear Sir: First of all I'd like to thank you for donating your suit. It fits fine, is exactly the right color for my eyes, complexion, and hair, but we have no use for the car keys found in the pants pocket so they are being returned herewith. Gratefully yours."

❖   ❖   ❖

Out in Phoenix, a maid mixed up the remainder of a box of weight-reducing cookies with a carton of dog biscuits. Her mistress finished the entire box before she became aware of the mistake. Any ill effects? Not really. I understand she didn't lose any weight, but she's barking better!

❖   ❖   ❖

A pullman porter, working in a car full of sleeping passengers headed for New York, stepped into the next car to shine his passengers' shoes while he chatted with another porter in a car headed for Atlanta. The switch was made before he realized his boo-boo and when the train arrived in

New York scores of curious folks turned around to stare and wonder why some 85 people were pounding through Pennsylvania Station in their stockings.

❖ ❖ ❖

Speaking of mistakes, Peter Lind Hayes wonders if we read this item in the *Buffalo News*. After several weeks of enjoying the eye-filling scenery from the window of his own bathroom, a neighbor in a new housing project decided to tell the girl next door that she'd better pull the shades when she took a shower. Investigation disclosed that the one-way glass in her bathroom window had been put in backwards.

❖ ❖ ❖

This one actually happened in suburban Long Island. A group of strikers were assigned to picket the home of an employer fighting union demands. Overly enthusiastic about their mission, the pickets trampled down all the flowerbeds in front of the house, ruined the lawn, and littered the flagstone sidewalks with chewing gum. Then they discovered they had made a slight error. They were picketing the home of their union president.

❖ ❖ ❖

Elaine and Dick Rubin, while in London, noticed this announcement in the personal columns: "Due to unforeseen circumstances the Clairvoyant Society of Charing Cross will not hold its weekly meeting this month."

❖ ❖ ❖

In Warrenton, N.C., according to Mickey Spillane, a group of bootleggers thought they fooled the local sheriff when they poured their white lightnin' down the drain as the place was raided. What they didn't figure on was a deputy who stood in the yard with a pitcher and caught the illegal hooch as it flowed down the drain.

❖   ❖   ❖

I can vouch for this "mistake" story for the simple reason that the columnist concerned is yours truly. Gene Leone, creator of one of the most successful restaurants in the country, took time out from his usual 24-hour day to deliver personally an armful of flowers to the Central Park South apartment of a columnist friend. The elevator operator insisted that Gene take the service entrance and rather than waste time arguing he did so. On his way out, Leone went first class and was harangued all the way down the 16 floors by the operator, who shook his head, repeating, "I don't have to do this, you know, I don't have to do this." Finally, as the lift approached the street floor, Gene chided his heckler: "I'm afraid that with your attitude you'll always be an elevator boy." "And you," the uniformed man snapped back at the millionaire, "will always be a delivery boy!"

16

Ask the Man
Who Owns One

TRUTH is stranger than fiction. And nowhere is the truth harder to swallow than in the little items newspaper editors digest with relish because they fit so snugly into little empty boxes tucked between news of more moment. With more cars on the road than there are people, and more people driving than walking, I suppose the category of cars creates more filler oddities than any subject but sex and mayhem.

❖ ❖ ❖

Before we unwrap some of the plums we plucked from the newspaper's morgue, I'd like to spin the true tale of a souped-up Volkswagen because it's one of the most incredible ribs ever pulled off on an unsuspecting victim. We'll keep the victim's name out of the yarn because he's already been tangled up enough in embarrassment. But we will reveal the name of the practical joker who engineered the dastardly deed.

Harry Morton is a reformed comedian who turned comedy writer and now is associated with comedian Jan Murray. His chief occupation, however, is misrepresentation. Harry is one of the most infamous practical jokers in show business. Yet he carries off his insane nightmares with such aplomb even his closest friends aren't aware of what he is up to until it is too late to stop him.

Recently a friend of Mr. Morton's bragged about how much mileage he was getting out of his new Volkswagen. Not one to discourage happiness in his set, Harry made certain his friend would really have something to brag about.

For more than six weeks, whenever the proud owner parked his car, Harry or an accomplice would slip into his private garage and fill the tank full of gas. The driver became thrilled, excited, and in time ecstatic. "This business of getting three to four hundred miles per gallon is remarkable," he'd whisper, incredulously. "I haven't had to fill the tank since I bought the car. I guess the American press suppresses information like this, afraid the American cars couldn't compete." Morton nodded agreement, finally wearied of the gag and reversed the procedure. Whenever his friend had the tank filled, Morton would furtively see to it that it was siphoned down to the point where the car would stop running after a few blocks.

Just a few days ago the Volkswagen owner got discouraged and drove the car back to his dealer. "Look, fellers," he said, "I'm not complaining. Like everyone else for a while there I was getting my 3 to 4 hundred miles to the gallon. But lately there must be a leak or a clogged up line or something. I keep filling up the tank and after a few blocks I keep running out of fuel. I wonder if you'd check this thing for me and give me a report?"

The boys at the dealer's service station, apprised in advance of their customer's "problem," said they'd give the Volkswagen a thorough going-over and call him when the car was ready to roll again. I imagine by now he's not only been called but realizes he's been had by an expert.

❖　　❖　　❖

One fellow who isn't bragging is a Miami traffic cop named Lewis J. Branning. While he was writing out a summons, the driver kept up such a running stream of conversation that the cop wrote his own name instead of the offender's on the ticket. The mistake came to light in traffic court—a red light, because all conversation stopped on a dime while everyone, including the genial officer, chuckled sheepishly.

❖　　❖　　❖

In California, where anything (well, almost anything) can happen, police arrested a woman for driving in heavy traffic while wearing a plastic bag draped over her head to keep her hair tidy. She claimed it was transparent, asked the judge to try it on for himself, he did, and promptly dismissed the charge of reckless driving. The woman thanked him, put the bag over her head again, and continued her trip while the magistrate closed court for the day. (This method of keeping hair tidy is not recommended. Even with holes cut for eyes and mouth it is flirting with suffocation.)

❖   ❖   ❖

In Idaho Falls, police stopping a truck that was weaving from side to side discovered an unlicensed driver at the wheel—a collie dog. (His bark was worse than the cop's bite!)

❖   ❖   ❖

Bewildering mixup in Baton Rouge: A visitor became so confused with the city's traffic signals he telephoned police headquarters to ask how to get to the state capitol. When asked where he was calling from, he looked around, then reported: "I'm at the corner of 'WALK' and 'DON'T WALK!'" (For all we know, he's still there.)

❖   ❖   ❖

Another chap to tangle with the police was a motorist named Johnson, who was so incensed at being fined $2 for parking overnight in a restricted area that he made out the check to the "West Hartford (Conn.) Police Gestapo." The court accepted the check, after fining him an additional $50 for his inelegant allusion to the local gendarme.

❖   ❖   ❖

Out in San Francisco, plagued with parking tickets, a local citizen had the time of his life. Taking a hammer in hand,

he went down the line and smashed the little glass **windows**
out of 138 parking meters!

❖   ❖   ❖

In a benevolent mood, rather than for the sake of retribu-
tion, a well-meaning inebriate strolled along a residential
area of Montreal jammed with illegally parked cars, and
ripped up all the traffic tickets strung to windshield wipers.
He explained he was just an old Boy Scout doing his good
deed for the day. The "good deed" cost him a $50 fine.

❖   ❖   ❖

And in Dayton, Ohio, another good samaritan had **signs**
printed and hung on dozens of parking meters reading:
"This Meter Out of Order." They weren't. But he was—for
ten days.

❖   ❖   ❖

Speaking of parking meters, in Chester, Ill., a river boat-
man actually received a ticket for tying his boat to a meter
during a flood without dropping in a coin.

❖   ❖   ❖

But the prize filler of them all concerned an Oakland, Calif., housewife named Marshall who took no chances. When she parked alongside a meter that required repairs, she attached a note reading: "Please fix meter. I spent hour at dentist having tooth pulled." Attached to the note with a piece of sticky tape was a coin—and the guilty tooth!

❖   ❖   ❖

Ontario police checked the driver of an illegally parked cab and discovered he was receiving a pension from the Canadian National Institute for the Blind.

❖   ❖   ❖

In Reading, Pa., a smiling, coy young lady in her middle flirties, handed the court clerk a parking ticket and said, "I'm returning this invitation. I found it hanging on my windshield by mistake."

❖   ❖   ❖

This one was unique enough to make the front page of the dignified *New York Herald Tribune*. Datelined, Rochester, N.Y., it was an AP dispatch which we'll reprint verbatim. "The wife of William B. Ransco has taken out another permit to learn to drive. Mr. Ransco believes the public should be properly alerted. He inserted this classified ad:

'NOTICE IS HEREBY GIVEN THAT MY DEAR WIFE HAS PURCHASED STILL ANOTHER DRIVER'S PERMIT. THE GUIDED MISSILE IS A '56 GREY CHEVROLET. PLEASE EXERCISE EXTREME CAUTION.' "

(We looked for and weren't too surprised not to see a follow-up front page story after Mrs. Ransco read Bill's ad. Which leads us to assume that the Rochester man has his wife Buffalo'd.)

❖   ❖   ❖

Joey Adams, who was an intimate friend of the late Mayor "Butch" LaGuardia, actually was present when the city's chief executive gave a police car driver a ticket for obstructing traffic at the scene of a fire.

❖   ❖   ❖

Down around the Federal Court area an attorney, in a rush to plead a case, parked his car too close to a hydrant and scribbled this sign: "Lawyer—on business inside." When he returned several hours later a summons was attached to his sign, with this postscript: "Cop—on business outside."

❖   ❖   ❖

In Greenville, Miss., John Haney made a slight mistake. His car rammed the rear of a parked car, the stationary vehicle belonging to the local sheriff. The latter was on the scene investigating a previous wreck.

❖   ❖   ❖

Though traffic and highway accidents continued to mount, it was 20 years ago that Harry Hershfield had the soundest idea for solving both problems. He suggested taking off the road all the cars that haven't been fully paid for.

❖   ❖   ❖

Asked why he was such a careful driver, a Washington hackie told his curious passenger, "It ain't like the old days, bud. Nowadays when you hit them pedestrians it's no fun filling out all those redtape forms."

❖   ❖   ❖

And in Philadelphia a hackie was being complimented by a fare for being such a proud father, hanging baby booties, children's pictures, and a rattle on his dashboard. "To tell the truth, mister," the cabbie chuckled, "that's just for the tourists. Akshelly, I'm a bachelor, but those props make folks think like you think and the father stuff gets me bigger tips."

❖   ❖   ❖

This incident proves that courtesy pays dividends. In Portland, Ore., a driver stopped his car to help a stalled motorist repair a flat tire. Before completing his chore he hailed a passing cop's car and told the officer he just recognized the stalled car as the one stolen from his wife just a few days previously.

❖   ❖   ❖

And this one appeared in Hal Eaton's *Long Island Star* column. In Long Island City, used car dealer Jerry Freeman bathed a shiny 1954 Lincoln convertible under a spotlight with the sign: "For $350 This Is a Steal." Which is exactly what it turned out to be. When Jerry wasn't looking somebody stole it.

❖   ❖   ❖

One police officer's ears still ring when he recalls this incident. A Port Washington, Wis., motorist sued Ozaukee County for $600, claiming he was forced to purchase a hearing aid after a motorcycle cop pulled alongside him and blew his siren so loud it deafened him.

❖   ❖   ❖

And to prove that honesty is the best policy, we'll wrap up the chapter with this note from a Des Moines newspaper. A woman who got a driver's license seven years ago became so unnerved when a tree drove into her car she gave up driving entirely. However, she renewed her license annually and recently received a citation and an invitation from the Iowa Safety Council to join the Good Drivers Club.

17

This Is the Absolute End

LATELY we've been inundated by "sick comedians." We've had sick jokes, sick humor, sick monologists who respect no one, dead or alive. Whether these so-called entertainers ever achieve any degree of stardom depends entirely upon how many Beatniks they can rally 'round the cause. Usually the bearded slobs, a form of description given to the beat degeneration, are so broke they can't afford to patronize any crib in which a sick comic performs. They must wait until he gets on tevee, which is sick enough without their painful presence.

This obviously is the age of sick entertainment. The popularity of all the spook movies knocking comedy and other shows for a ghoul in TV ratings underscores the point. In any event, we thought we'd inject a chapter reflecting the era, one in which we will attempt to prove that there's even a touch of pathetic humor in the field of the mortician. Myron Cohen, for example, told of an eerie experience he had working at Belden Katelman's El Rancho Vegas in Las

Vegas. The storyteller was almost afraid to start talking when he learned that his entire audience consisted of undertakers on a convention. By the time he was through he summed up his experience by telling the audience that they were the warmest, most responsive group of people he had had the pleasure of entertaining in many months. "This is the first time," he concluded, "that I ever saw so many undertakers laughing at somebody who was alive."

❖   ❖   ❖

Still in Las Vegas, I'd like to repeat a story *Sun* publisher Hank Greenspun likes to tell visitors. It concerns a croupier who belonged in the top echelon of society in the gambling city, but who was caught cheating and fired on the spot. Since gambling is legalized in Nevada and there are no phony bust-out games, anyone violating the code of honesty is ostracized. Unable to work in any casino in town, the disgraced croupier finally took a job as night watchman in a funeral parlor. One evening a group of his friends visited with the unhappy man and noticed that there were bodies lying on all 12 slabs. "Business is up to capacity," one of them commented, "isn't it?" "No," the one-time gambler shrugged. "Don't let those slabs fool you. Half of those bodies are shills."

❖   ❖   ❖

My friend Myles Lane, the former U.S. attorney and the first chairman of the New York State Crime Commission, who sent a group of the Apalachin conferees to the hoosegow, related an interesting incident that occurred in the Bronx. Two men insisted to the court that they bought the same cemetery plot and both tried to prove ownership. The magistrate finally solved the problem to everybody's satisfaction. Said he: "Whoever dies first, gets it."

❖   ❖   ❖

Bernie Miller passes along a whole group of odd names of people obviously in the right business. These include a fellow named Kroak, a funeral director in Stephan, Minn.; Boxwell Brothers funeral directors in Austin, Texas; G. Ima Gonnar, a mortician in Buffalo, N.Y.; the undertaking parlor of Dye and Berry of Hot Springs, N. Mex.; I. Laidlow, who lays them low in Hurleyville, N.Y.; J. Posthumous, an undertaker in Grand Rapids, Mich. Unquestionably the fellow who has the most fun in his business is a mortician in Anniston, Ala. His shingle reads: "I. N. Joy, UNDERTAKING."

❖   ❖   ❖

In many cities local radio and TV stations are perfectly willing to accept the advertising of mortuaries despite the fact that such announcements are incongruous when spotted between comedy or musical shows. As an example, an Austin, Texas, radio station turned down an offer from a local funeral parlor to buy a one-minute commercial before and after a Lux Theater dramatic show titled "Nobody Lives Forever."

❖   ❖   ❖

Herb Lyons, the noted columnist of the *Chicago Tribune,* came up with an interesting observation. The Banquet Department of one of the city's most famous hotels has a stuffed figure which they call Louis XIV. Louis is seated at intimate banquets when only 13 people show up and the folks who run the affair are superstitious.

❖   ❖   ❖

I don't know whether it's the television influence, but I understand that there's a movie theater in Moose, N. Dak., that finds it can make more money running only evening performances. Since it's an economic waste for the theater to remain empty during the daylight hours, from 9 a.m. until 5 p.m. the premises are rented out for use as a funeral parlor.

❖   ❖   ❖

We've heard of courtesy, but I think that George N. Smith of Buckland, Mo., went a little too far when he was on his death bed. He spent $7.50 to advertise in the local newspaper that the reason he wasn't able to send all his friends thank you notes for get-well notes was that he was much too occupied dying.

❖   ❖   ❖

This belongs in the category of sick jokes, I suppose. Anyway, it has its amusing aspects. A bunch of the boys were whooping it up at the African Room in New York when the talk got around to a dope peddler who was buried that morning. "They gave Buz a real important funeral," one fellow said. "Even Mr. X was sad, saying he was one of the best pushers we ever had." "Ain't that life," the other said, shaking his head. "You gotta die before they say something nice about you!"

❖   ❖   ❖

And then there was the chap in California who explained to Santa Monica police why he attempted to end his life. "While driving along the mountain road," he explained, "I saw a billboard advertising a complete funeral for $110, so I thought I might as well die before I spent the money on something foolish."

❖   ❖   ❖

Which brings to mind the mortician in Los Angeles who has spent hundreds of thousands of dollars advertising the slogan "Go Now, Pay Later."

❖   ❖   ❖

I hope that Frank Koss, a World War II veteran of Austin, Texas, is still alive. Not that I ever met Frank, but I like his stubbornness. On three different occasions he refused to believe a telegram he got from the War Department advising him that he was dead.

❖   ❖   ❖

I'll admit that this is one item I lifted straight from my own column during a strike of grave diggers in the New York area. The item quoted the motto printed on the stationery of the grave diggers' union—"We're the last ones to let you down." (For the relatives of the poor souls who died and were about to be buried during the strike, it was suggested that the grave diggers change their slogan to read: "Here's mud in your eyes!")

❖   ❖   ❖

Then there's a Pennsylvania cemetery tombstone reading: "Persons are prohibited picking flowers from any but their own graves."

❖   ❖   ❖

You can take or leave this one. I choose to accept its veracity even though I'll admit the incident taxes the imagination. In Detroit, a car thief stole a trunkful of clothes from out of the parked vehicle of a traveling salesman. What the thief didn't know was that the hot dresses and suits were burial clothes for sale to undertakers. A small notice in the papers the following day pointed out this interesting bit of intelligence. That anyone purchasing such a load of merchandise from a stranger should beware of one thing. The men's suits are strictly one sided, that burial clothes, in this instance at least, covered only the front portion of the body. . . .

❖　❖　❖

Mike Wallace met up with an interesting clergyman on his interview show. Asked whether he preferred to officiate at a wedding or a funeral, the man of the cloth thought a moment, then replied: "I guess I prefer to officiate at funerals. At least then I know their troubles are over."

❖　❖　❖

Another odd name for an odd business. The local tombstone cutter in Viroqua, Wis., is named Graves—Robert Graves. And when a member of a bowling club in Ft. Lauderdale, Fla., passed away, he left $25 in his will so his pallbearers could have a round of drinks on him. If you doubt whether this actually happened I refer you to the owner of the bowling alleys, Rocky Marciano, the undefeated and retired heavyweight champion of the world!

❖　❖　❖

Some quickies: A Norwich, Conn., hearse bears the license "U-2." And a sign near Burlington, Vt., purchased by an undertaking firm, reads: "Haste Makes WAKES." And in Waterbury, Conn., a local embalmer endears himself to his neighbors with this slogan: "You arrange the day; we do the rest."

❖　❖　❖

One of the silliest reasons for the cancellation of an order to buy a plot occurred in a Newark cemetery when a chap explained, "I notice that my plot is near a lake and that's undesirable—it would affect my rheumatism."

❖ ❖ ❖

This one comes from Joe E. Lewis. He knew a chap named Stocky Kane, a fellow horse bettor from Albany, N.Y. In accordance with his last wishes, when Stocky died he was cremated and his ashes were scattered over the last stretch of the Saratoga race track.

❖ ❖ ❖

Undoubtedly, the most thoughtful of all recent accident victims was a gentleman from London named Albert Woodey. Woodey, who almost died from pneumonia after catching a bad cold when he stood bare headed in the rain at the funeral services of a friend, asked in his will that friends at his funeral please keep their hats on so that they wouldn't catch pneumonia.